Nelson's *Bedtime Bible Stories*

From the
icb International Children's Bible®

Illustrated by
Paul Gross

THOMAS NELSON BIBLES
A Division of Thomas Nelso
www.ThomasNelso

Table of Contents

New Testament

About the Gospels—the Stories of Jesus' Life and Work

Matthew

John

Acts

Revelation

How Did the Bible Come to Us?

The Bible is an amazing book. There is so much in it that can help you make good choices, help you deal with the tough things happening in your life, and help you become a better follower of Jesus. And it is all in one book!

The word "Bible" comes from the Greek word *biblia,* which means "books." So the Bible is really a collection of many books by 40 writers. The Holy Spirit gave the authors God's thoughts to write down. That's called inspiration! These books are divided into two main parts, the Old Testament and the New Testament.

The books in the Old Testament were written in Hebrew and tell the history of the people of Israel from the beginning of time to about 400 B.C. (400 years before Jesus came). The Old Testament books talk about the person God promised to send to help people, the person called the Messiah.

The coming of this Messiah, Jesus Christ, is described in the New Testament. The 27 books in the New Testament were written in Greek by the followers of Jesus Christ, from about A.D. 30 to A.D. 65 (30 to 65 years after Jesus came to earth). Over the years, Bible scholars have spent billions

of hours translating the Bible—that is, changing the words from one language to another. Today we have more than 24 modern translations we can use to read the words of God.

Nelson's Bedtime Bible Stories is a collection of 150 exciting stories straight from the pages of the Bible. These stories help you get to know some of the many different people in God's Word. These stories also tell of God's love for his people and his work in their lives. As you read, you will discover wonderful things about who God is and how he wants you to live.

OLD TESTAMENT

The Story of Creation

(From Genesis 1 and 2)

1:¹In the beginning God created the sky and the earth. ²The earth was empty and had no form. Darkness covered the ocean, and God's Spirit was moving over the water.

³Then God said, "Let there be light!" And there was light. ⁴ᵇHe divided the light from the darkness. ⁵God named the light "day" and the darkness "night." Evening passed, and morning came. This was the first day.

⁶Then God said, "Let there be something to divide the water in two!" ⁷So God made the air to divide the water in two. Some of the water was above the air, and some of the water was below it. ⁸God named the air "sky." Evening passed, and morning came. This was the second day.

⁹ᵃThen God said, "Let the water under the sky be gathered together so the dry land will appear." ¹⁰God named the dry land "earth." He named the water that was gathered together "seas." God saw that this was good.

¹¹Then God said, "Let the earth produce plants. . . ." And it happened. ¹³Evening passed, and morning came. This was the third day.

¹⁴ᵃThen God said, "Let there be lights in the sky to separate day from night." ¹⁶So God made the two large lights. He made the brighter light to rule the day. He made the smaller light to rule the night. He also made the stars. ¹⁸ᵇGod saw that all these things were good. ¹⁹Evening passed, and morning came. This was the fourth day.

²⁰Then God said, "Let the water be filled with living things. And let birds fly in the air above the earth." ²¹ᵃSo God created the large sea animals. He created every living thing that moves in the sea. . . . God also made every bird that flies. ²³Evening passed, and morning came. This was the fifth day.

²⁴Then God said, "Let the earth be filled with animals. And let each produce more of its own kind. Let there be tame animals and small crawling animals and wild animals. And let each produce more of its kind." And it happened.

²⁶ᵃThen God said, "Let us make human beings in our image and likeness." ²⁷So God created human beings in his image. In the image of God he created them. He created them male and female. ²⁸ᵃGod blessed them and said, "Have many children and grow in number. Fill the earth and be its master."

³¹God looked at everything he had made, and it was very good. Evening passed, and morning came. This was the sixth day.

2:¹So the sky, the earth and all that filled them were finished. ²By the seventh day God finished the work he had been doing. So on the seventh day he rested from all his work. ³God blessed the seventh day and made it a holy day. He made it holy because on that day he rested. He rested from all the work he had done in creating the world.

Adam and Eve Disobey God
(From Genesis 3)

3:¹Now the snake was the most clever of all the wild animals the Lord God had made. One day the snake spoke to the woman. He said, "Did God really say that you must not eat fruit from any tree in the garden?"

²The woman answered the snake, "We may eat fruit from the trees in the garden. ³But God told us, 'You must not eat fruit from the tree that is in the middle of the garden. You must not even touch it, or you will die.'"

⁴But the snake said to the woman, "You will not die. ⁵God knows that if you eat the fruit from that tree, you will learn about good and evil. Then you will be like God!"

⁶The woman saw that the tree was beautiful. She saw that its fruit was good to eat and that it would make her wise. So she took some of its fruit and ate it. She also gave some of the fruit to her husband, and he ate it.

[7]Then, it was as if the man's and woman's eyes were opened. They realized they were naked. So they sewed fig leaves together and made something to cover themselves. [8]Then they heard the Lord God walking in the garden. This was during the cool part of the day. And the man and his wife hid from the Lord God among the trees in the garden. [9]But the Lord God called to the man. The Lord said, "Where are you?"

[10]The man answered, "I heard you walking in the garden. I was afraid because I was naked. So I hid."

[11]God said to the man, "Who told you that you were naked? Did you eat fruit from that tree? I commanded you not to eat from that tree."

[12]The man said, "You gave this woman to me. She gave me fruit from the tree. So I ate it."

[13]Then the Lord God said to the woman, "What have you done?"

She answered, "The snake tricked me. So I ate the fruit."

[14a]The Lord God said to the snake,
"Because you did this,
    a curse will be put on you."

[16a]Then God said to the woman,
"I will cause you to have much trouble . . .
    when you give birth to children."

4

17aThen God said to the man, "You listened to what your wife said. And you ate fruit from the tree that I commanded you not to eat from.

"So I will put a curse on the ground. You will have to work very hard for food."

21The Lord God made clothes from animal skins for the man and his wife. And so the Lord dressed them. 22Then the Lord God said, "Look, the man has become like one of us. He knows good and evil. And now we must keep him from eating some of the fruit from the tree of life. If he does, he will live forever." 23aSo the Lord God forced the man out of the garden of Eden.

Cain and Abel

(From Genesis 4)

4:1[Eve] . . . became pregnant and gave birth to Cain. Eve said, "With the Lord's help, I have given birth to a man." 2After that, Eve gave birth to Cain's brother Abel. Abel took care of sheep. Cain became a farmer.

3Later, Cain brought a gift to God. He brought some food from the ground. 4Abel brought the best parts of his best sheep. The Lord accepted Abel and his gift. 5But God did not accept Cain and his gift. Cain became very angry and looked unhappy.

6The Lord asked Cain, "Why are you angry? Why do you look so unhappy? 7If you do good, I will accept you. But if you do not do good, sin is ready to attack you. Sin wants you. But you must rule over it."

⁸Cain said to his brother Abel, "Let's go out into the field." So Cain and Abel went into the field. Then Cain attacked his brother Abel and killed him.

⁹Later, the Lord said to Cain, "Where is your brother Abel?"

Cain answered, "I don't know. Is it my job to take care of my brother?"

¹⁰Then the Lord said, "What have you done? Your brother's blood is on the ground. That blood is like a voice that tells me what happened. ¹¹And now you will be cursed in your work with the ground. It is the same ground where your brother's blood fell. Your hands killed him. ¹²You will work the ground. But it will not grow good crops for you anymore. You will wander around on the earth."

¹³Then Cain said to the Lord, "This punishment is more than I can stand! ¹⁴Look! You have forced me to stop working the ground. And now I must hide from you. I will wander around on the earth. And anyone who meets me can kill me."

¹⁵Then the Lord said to Cain, "No! If anyone kills you, I will punish that person seven times more." Then the Lord put a mark on Cain. It was a warning to anyone who met him not to kill him.

Noah and the Flood

(From Genesis 6—9)

6:[9b]Noah was a good man. He was the most innocent man of his time. He walked with God. [10]Noah had three sons: Shem, Ham and Japheth.

[11]People on earth did what God said was evil. Violence was everywhere. [12]And God saw this evil. All people on the earth did only evil. [13]So God said to Noah, "People have made the earth full of violence. So I will destroy all people from the earth. [14]Build a boat of cypress wood for yourself. Make rooms in it and cover it inside and outside with tar. [17]I will bring a flood of water on the earth. I will destroy all living things that live under the sky. This includes everything that has the breath of life. Everything on the earth will die. [18]But I will make an agreement with you. You, your sons, your wife and your sons' wives will all go into the boat. [19]Also, you must bring into the boat two of every living thing, male and female. Keep them alive with you.

[22]Noah did everything that God commanded him.

7:[7]He and his wife and his sons and their wives went into the boat. They went in to escape the waters of the flood. [8]The . . . animals . . . [9a]went into the boat. [10]Seven days later the flood started. [12]The rain fell on the earth for 40 days and 40 nights. [19]The water rose so much that even the highest mountains under the sky were covered by it. [22a]So everything on dry land died. [23b]All that was left was Noah and what was with him in the boat. [24]And the waters continued to cover the earth for 150 days.

8:[1a]But God remembered Noah and all the wild animals and tame animals with him in the boat. God made a wind blow over the earth. [3–4a]The water that covered the earth began to go down. After 150 days the water had gone down so much that the boat touched land again. It came to rest on one of the mountains of Ararat.

[8]Then Noah sent out a dove. This was to find out if the water had dried up from the ground. [9a]The dove could not find a place to land because water still covered the earth. So it came back to the boat.

[10]After seven days Noah again sent out the dove from the boat. [11a]And that evening it came back to him with a fresh olive leaf in its mouth. [12]Seven

days later he sent the dove out again. But this time it did not come back.

¹⁵Then God said to Noah, ¹⁶"You and your wife, your sons and their wives should go out of the boat. ¹⁷ᵃBring every animal out of the boat with you."

9:⁸Then God said to Noah and his sons, ⁹"Now I am making my agreement with you and your people who will live after you. ¹⁰ᵃAnd I also make it with every living thing that is with you. ¹¹ᵇI will never again destroy all living things by flood-waters. A flood will never again destroy the earth.

¹³"I am putting my rainbow in the clouds. It is the sign of the agreement between me and the earth. ¹⁴When I bring clouds over the earth, a rainbow appears in the clouds. ¹⁵ᵃThen I will remember my agreement."

The Tower of Babel

(From Genesis 11)

11:¹At this time the whole world spoke one language. Everyone used the same words. ²As people moved from the East, they found a plain in the land of Babylonia. They settled there to live.

³They said to each other, "Let's make bricks and bake them to make them hard." So they used bricks instead of stones, and tar instead of mortar. ⁴Then they said to each other, "Let's build for ourselves a city and a tower. And let's make the top of the tower reach high into the sky. We will become

9

famous. If we do this, we will not be scattered over all the earth."

⁵The Lord came down to see the city and the tower that the people had built. ⁶The Lord said, "Now, these people are united. They all speak the same language. This is only the beginning of what they will do. They will be able to do anything they want. ⁷Come, let us go down and confuse their language. Then they will not be able to understand each other."

⁸So the Lord scattered them from there over all the earth. And they stopped building the city. ⁹That is where the Lord confused the language of the whole world. So the place is called Babel. So the Lord caused them to spread out from there over all the whole world.

Abram Obeys God

(From Genesis 11—13, 15)

11:²⁶ After Terah [a descendant of Shem] was 70 years old, his sons Abram, Nahor and Haran were born.

²⁸Haran died while his father, Terah, was still

10

alive. This happened in Ur in Babylonia, where he was born. ²⁹ᵃAbram and Nahor both married. Abram's wife was named Sarai. ³⁰Sarai was not able to have children.

³¹Terah took his son Abram, his grandson Lot (Haran's son) and his daughter-in-law Sarai (Abram's wife). They moved out of Ur of Babylonia. They had planned to go to the land of Canaan. But when they reached the city of Haran, they settled there.

12:¹Then the Lord said to Abram, "Leave your country, your relatives and your father's family. Go to the land I will show you.

²I will make you a great nation,
   and I will bless you.
 I will make you famous.
   And you will be a blessing to others.
³I will bless those who bless you.
   I will place a curse on those who harm you.
 And all the people on earth
   will be blessed through you."

⁴ᵃSo Abram left Haran as the Lord had told him. ⁵ᵃAbram took his wife Sarai, his nephew Lot and everything they owned. They took all the servants they had gotten in Haran.

13:²Abram was very rich in cattle, silver and gold.

⁵During this time Lot was traveling with Abram. Lot also had many sheep, cattle and tents. ⁶Abram and Lot had so many animals that the land could not support both of them together. ⁷ᵃAbram's herders and Lot's herders began to argue.

⁸So Abram said to Lot, "There should be no arguing between you and me. Your herders and mine should not argue either. We are brothers. ⁹We should separate. The whole land is there in front of you. If you go to the left, I will go to the right. If you go to the right, I will go to the left."

¹⁰ᵃLot looked all around and saw the whole Jordan Valley. He saw that there was much water there. ¹¹So Lot chose to move east and live in the Jordan Valley. In this way Abram and Lot separated.

15:⁵Then God led Abram outside. God said, "Look at the sky. There are so many stars you cannot count them. And your descendants will be too many to count."

⁶Abram believed the Lord. And the Lord accepted Abram's faith, and that faith made him right with God.

¹⁸So . . . the Lord made an agreement with Abram. The Lord said, "I will give this land to your descendants. I will give them the land between the river of Egypt and the great river Euphrates."

The Promise of a Son

(From Genesis 17 and 18)

17:¹When Abram was 99 years old, the Lord appeared to him. The Lord said, "I am God All-Powerful. Obey me and do what is right. ²I will make an agreement between us. I will make you the ancestor of many people."

³Then Abram bowed facedown on the ground. God said to him, ⁴"I am making my agreement with you: I will make you the father of many nations. ⁵I am changing your name from Abram to Abraham. This is because I am making you a father of many nations. ⁶I will give you many descendants. New nations will be born from you. Kings will come from you. ⁸You live in the land of Canaan now as a stranger. But I will give you and your descendants all this land forever. And I will be the God of your descendants."

¹⁵God said to Abraham, "I will change the name of Sarai, your wife. Her new name will be Sarah. I will bless her. I will give her a son, and you will be the father. She will be the mother of many nations. Kings of nations will come from her."

18:¹Later, the Lord again appeared to Abraham near the great trees of Mamre. At that time Abraham was sitting at the door of his tent. It was during the hottest part of the day. ²He looked up and saw three men standing near him. When Abraham saw them, he ran from his tent to meet them. He bowed facedown on the ground before them. ³Abraham said, "Sir, if you think well of me, please stay awhile with me, your servant. ⁴I will bring some water so all of you can wash your feet. You may rest under the tree. ⁵I will get some bread for you, so you can regain your strength. Then you may continue your journey."

The three men said, "That is fine. Do as you said."

⁸ᵇWhile the three men ate, [Abraham] stood under the tree near them.

⁹The men asked Abraham, "Where is your wife Sarah?"

"There, in the tent," said Abraham.

¹⁰Then the Lord said, "I will certainly return to you about this time a year from now. At that time your wife Sarah will have a son."

Sarah was listening at the entrance of the tent which was behind him. ¹¹Abraham and Sarah were very old. Sarah was past the age when women normally have children. ¹²So she laughed to herself, "My husband and I are too old to have a baby."

¹³Then the Lord said to Abraham, "Why did Sarah laugh? Why did she say, 'I am too old to have a baby'? ¹⁴Is anything too hard for the Lord? No! I will return to you at the right time a year from now. And Sarah will have a son."

Sodom and Gomorrah

(From Genesis 18 and 19)

18:²⁰Then the Lord said, "I have heard many things against the people of Sodom and Gomorrah. They are very evil. ²¹So I will go down and see if they are as bad as I have heard." . . .

19:¹The two angels came to Sodom in the evening. Lot was sitting near the city gate and saw them. He got up and went to them and bowed face-down on the ground. ²Lot said, "Sirs, please come to my house and spend the night. There you can wash your feet. Then tomorrow you may continue your journey."

^{3b}They agreed and went to his house. . . . ⁴Before bedtime, all the men of the city surrounded Lot's house. These men were both young and old and came from every part of Sodom. ^{5a}They called to Lot, "Where are the two men who came to you tonight? Bring them out to us."

⁶Lot went outside to them, closing the door behind him. ^{7a}He said, "No, my brothers! ^{8b}Please don't do anything to these men. They have come to my house, and I must protect them."

⁹The men around the house answered, "Move out of the way!" . . . So they started pushing Lot back. They were ready to break down the door.

¹⁰But the two men staying with Lot opened the door and pulled him back inside the house. Then they closed the door. ¹¹The two men struck the men outside the door with blindness. So these men, both young and old, could not find the door.

¹²The two men said to Lot, "Do you have any other

relatives in this city? . . . If you do, tell them to leave now. ¹³ᵃWe are about to destroy this city."

¹⁵At dawn the next morning, the angels begged Lot to hurry. They said, "Go! Take your wife and your two daughters with you. Then you will not be destroyed when the city is punished."

¹⁶But Lot delayed. So the two men took the hands of Lot, his wife and his two daughters. The men led them safely out of the city. So the Lord was merciful to Lot and his family. ¹⁷The two men brought Lot and his family out of the city. Then one of the men said, "Run for your lives! Don't look back or stop . . . or you will be destroyed."

²⁴The Lord sent a rain of burning sulfur down from the sky on Sodom and Gomorrah. ²⁵ᵃSo the Lord destroyed those cities.

²⁶At that point Lot's wife looked back. When she did, she became a pillar of salt.

God Makes a Promise to Ishmael

(From Genesis 21)

21:¹The Lord cared for Sarah as he had said. He did for her what he had promised. ²Sarah became pregnant. And she gave birth to a son for Abraham in his old age. Everything happened at the time God had said it would. ³Abraham named his son Isaac. Sarah gave birth to this son of Abraham.

⁸Isaac grew and became old enough to eat food. At that time Abraham gave a great feast. ⁹But Sarah saw Ishmael making fun of Isaac. (Ishmael was the son of Abraham by Hagar, Sarah's Egyptian slave.) ¹⁰So Sarah said to Abraham, "Throw out this slave woman and her son. When we die, our son Isaac will inherit everything we have. I don't want her son to inherit any of our things."

¹¹This troubled Abraham very much because Ishmael was also his son. ¹²But God said to Abraham, "Don't be troubled about the boy and the slave woman. Do whatever Sarah tells you. The descendants I promised you will be from Isaac. ¹³I will also make the descendants of Ishmael into a great nation. I will do this because he is your son, too."

¹⁴Early the next morning Abraham took some food and a leather bag full of water. He gave them to Hagar and sent her away. Hagar carried these things and her son. She went and wandered in the desert of Beersheba.

¹⁵Later, all the water was gone from the bag. So Hagar put her son under a bush.

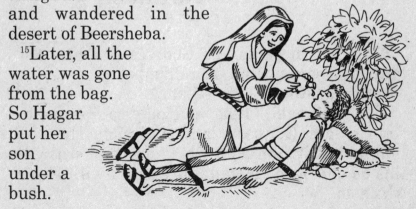

¹⁶Then she went away a short distance and sat down. Hagar thought, "My son will die. I cannot watch this happen." She sat there and began to cry.

¹⁷God heard the boy crying. And God's angel called to Hagar from heaven. He said, "What is wrong, Hagar? Don't be afraid! God has heard the boy crying there. ¹⁸Help the boy up. Take him by the hand. I will make his descendants into a great nation."

¹⁹Then God showed Hagar a well of water. So she went to the well and filled her bag with water. Then she gave the boy a drink.

²⁰God was with the boy as he grew up. Ishmael lived in the desert. He learned to shoot with a bow very well. ²¹He lived in the Desert of Paran. His mother found a wife for him in Egypt.

God Tests Abraham

(From Genesis 22)

22:¹After these things God tested Abraham's faith. God said to him, "Abraham!"

And he answered, "Here I am."

²Then God said, "Take your only son, Isaac, the son you love. Go to the land of Moriah. There kill him and offer him as a whole burnt offering. Do this on one of the mountains there. I will tell you which one."

³Early in the morning Abraham got up and saddled his donkey. He took Isaac and two servants with him. He cut the wood for the sacrifice. Then they went to the place God had told them to go. ⁴On the third day Abraham looked up and saw the place in the distance. ⁵He said to his servants, "Stay here with the donkey. My son and I will go over there and worship. Then we will come back to you."

⁶Abraham took the wood for the sacrifice and gave it to his son to carry. Abraham took the knife and the fire. So Abraham and his son went on together.

⁷Isaac said to his father Abraham, "Father!"

Abraham answered, "Yes, my son."

Isaac said, "We have the fire and the wood. But where is the lamb we will burn as a sacrifice?"

⁸Abraham answered, "God will give us the lamb for the sacrifice, my son."

So Abraham and his son went on together. ⁹They came to the place God had told him about. There, Abraham built an altar. He laid the wood on it. Then he tied up his son Isaac. And he laid Isaac on the wood on the altar.

¹⁰Then Abraham took his knife and was about to kill his son.

¹¹But the angel of the Lord called to him from heaven. The angel said, "Abraham! Abraham!"

Abraham answered, "Yes."

¹²The angel said, "Don't kill

your son or hurt him in any way. Now I can see that you respect God. I see that you have not kept your son, your only son, from me."

¹³Then Abraham looked up and saw a male sheep. Its horns were caught in a bush. So Abraham went and took the sheep and killed it. He offered it as a whole burnt offering to God. Abraham's son was saved. ¹⁴So Abraham named that place The Lord Gives. Even today people say, "On the mountain of the Lord it will be given."

A Wife for Isaac
(From Genesis 24)

24:¹Abraham was now very old. The Lord had blessed him in every way. ²Abraham's oldest servant was in charge of everything Abraham owned. Abraham called that servant to him and said, " . . . ³Make a promise to me before the Lord, the God of heaven and earth. Don't get a wife for my son from the Canaanite girls who live around here. ⁴Instead, go back to my country, to the land of my relatives. Get a wife for my son Isaac from there."

⁹So the servant . . . made a promise to Abraham about this.

¹⁰The servant took ten of Abraham's camels and left. He carried with him many different kinds of beautiful gifts. He went to Northwest Mesopotamia to Nahor's city. ¹¹He made the camels kneel down at the well outside the city. It was in the evening when the women come out to get water.

[12]The servant said, "Lord, you are the God of my master Abraham. Allow me to find a wife for his son today. Please show this kindness to my master Abraham. [13]Here I am, standing by the spring of water. The girls from the city are coming out to get water. [14]I will say to one of the girls, 'Please put your jar down so I can drink.' Then let her say, 'Drink, and I will also give water to your camels.' If that happens, I will know she is the right one for your servant Isaac. And I will know that you have shown kindness to my master."

[15]Before the servant had finished praying, Rebekah came out of the city. She was the daughter of Bethuel. (Bethuel was the son of Milcah and Nahor, Abraham's brother.) Rebekah was carrying her water jar on her shoulder. [16]She was very pretty. . . . She went down to the spring and filled her jar. Then she came back up. [17]The servant ran to her and said, "Please give me a little water from your jar."

[18]Rebekah said, "Drink, sir." She quickly lowered the jar from her shoulder and gave him a drink. [19]After he finished drinking, Rebekah said, "I will also pour some water for your camels." [20]So she quickly poured all the water from her jar into the drinking trough for the camels. Then she kept running to the well until she had given all the camels enough to drink.

²¹The servant quietly watched her. He wanted to be sure the Lord had made his trip successful. ²²After the camels had finished drinking, he gave Rebekah a gold ring . . . [and] two gold arm bracelets. . . . ²³The servant asked, "Who is your father? Is there a place in his house for me and my men to spend the night?"

²⁴Rebekah answered, "My father is Bethuel. He is the son of Milcah and Nahor." ²⁵Then she said, "And, yes, we have straw for your camels. We have a place for you to spend the night."

²⁶The servant bowed and worshiped the Lord. ²⁷He said, "Blessed is the Lord, the God of my master Abraham. The Lord has been kind and truthful to him. He has led me to my master's relatives."

Jacob Tricks Esau

(From Genesis 25)

25:¹⁹This is the family history of Isaac. Abraham had a son named Isaac. ²⁰When Isaac was 40 years old, he married Rebekah. Rebekah was from Northwest Mesopotamia. She was Bethuel's daughter and the sister of Laban the Aramean. ²¹Isaac's wife could not have children. So Isaac prayed to the Lord for her. The Lord heard Isaac's prayer, and Rebekah became pregnant.

²²While she was pregnant, the babies struggled inside her. She asked, "Why is this happening to

me?" Then she went to get an answer from the Lord.

²³The Lord said to her,

"Two nations are in your body.
Two groups of people will be taken from you.
One group will be stronger than the other.
The older will serve the younger."

²⁴And when the time came, Rebekah gave birth to twins. ²⁵The first baby was born red. His skin was like a hairy robe. So he was named Esau. ²⁶When the second baby was born, he was holding on to Esau's heel. So that baby was named Jacob. Isaac was 60 years old when they were born.

²⁷When the boys grew up, Esau became a skilled hunter. He loved to be out in the fields. But Jacob was a quiet man. He stayed among the tents. ²⁸Isaac loved Esau. Esau hunted the wild animals that Isaac enjoyed eating. But Rebekah loved Jacob.

²⁹One day Jacob was boiling a pot of vegetable soup. Esau came in from hunting in the fields. He was weak from hunger. ³⁰So Esau said to Jacob, "Let me eat some of that red soup. I am weak with hunger." (That is why people call him Edom.)

³¹But Jacob said, "You must sell me your rights as the firstborn son."

³²Esau said, "I am almost dead from hunger. If I die, all of my father's wealth will not help me."

³³But Jacob said, "First, promise me that you will give it to me." So Esau made a promise to Jacob. In this way he sold his part of their father's wealth to Jacob. ³⁴Then Jacob gave Esau bread and vegetable soup. Esau ate and drank and then left. So Esau showed how little he cared about his rights as the firstborn son.

Jacob Tricks Isaac

(From Genesis 27 and 28)

27:¹ᵃWhen Isaac was old, his eyes were not good. He could not see clearly. One day he called his older son Esau to him. ²Isaac said, "I am old. I don't know when I might die. ³So . . . go hunting in the field. Kill an animal for me to eat. ⁴Prepare the tasty food that I love. Bring it to me, and I will eat. Then I will bless you before I die." ⁵So Esau went out in the field to hunt.

Rebekah was listening as Isaac said this to his son Esau. ⁶ᵃRebekah said to her son Jacob, ⁸" . . . Obey me, my son. Do what I tell you. ⁹Go out to our goats and bring me two young ones. I will prepare them just the way your father likes them. ¹⁰Then you will take the food to your father. And he will bless you before he dies."

¹⁴So Jacob went out and got two goats and

brought them to his mother. Then she cooked them in the special way Isaac enjoyed. ¹⁵She took the best clothes of her older son Esau. . . . She put them on the younger son Jacob. ¹⁶She took the skins of the goats. And she put them on Jacob's hands and neck.

¹⁸Jacob went in to his father. . . .

And his father said, "Yes, my son. Who are you?"

¹⁹ᵃJacob said to him, "I am Esau, your first son."

²¹Then Isaac said to Jacob, "Come near so I can touch you, my son. If I can touch you, I will know if you are really my son Esau."

²²So Jacob came near to Isaac his father. Isaac touched him and said, "Your voice sounds like Jacob's voice. But your hands are hairy like the hands of Esau." ²³ᵇSo Isaac blessed Jacob.

³⁰ᵇThen . . . Esau came in from hunting. ³¹Esau also prepared some tasty food and brought it to his father. He said, "Father, rise and eat the food that your son killed for you. Then bless me."

³²Isaac asked, "Who are you?"

He answered, "I am your son—your firstborn son—Esau."

³³Then Isaac trembled greatly. He said, "Then

who was it that . . . brought me food before you came? I ate it, and I blessed him. And it is too late now to take back my blessing."

[41a]After that Esau hated Jacob because of the blessing from Isaac.

[42]Rebekah . . . sent for Jacob. She said to him, "Listen, your brother Esau is . . . planning to kill you. [43]So, son, do what I say. My brother Laban is living in Haran. Go to him at once!"

28:[10]Jacob left Beersheba and set out for Haran. [11]He came to a place and spent the night there. . . . He found a stone there and laid his head on it to go to sleep. [12]Jacob dreamed that there was a ladder resting on the earth and reaching up into heaven. And he saw angels of God going up and coming down the ladder. [13]And then Jacob saw the Lord. . . . The Lord said, "I am the Lord, the God of Abraham your grandfather. And I am the God of Isaac. I will give you and your descendants the land on which you are now sleeping. [15a]I am with you, and I will protect you everywhere you go."

Jacob Finds a Wife

(From Genesis 29)

29:[1]Then Jacob continued his journey. He came to the land of the people of the East. [2]He looked and saw a well in the field. . . . A large stone covered the mouth of the well. [3]All the [area] flocks would gather there. The shepherds would roll the stone away from the well and water the sheep. Then they would put the stone back in its place.

⁴Jacob said to the shepherds there, "My brothers, where are you from?"

They answered, "We are from Haran."

⁵Then Jacob asked, "Do you know Laban grandson of Nahor?"

They answered, "We know him."

⁶Then Jacob asked, "How is he?"

They answered, "He is well. Look, his daughter Rachel is coming now with his sheep."

⁹While Jacob was talking with the shepherds, Rachel came with her father's sheep. It was her job to take care of the sheep. ¹⁰Then Jacob . . . went to the well and rolled the stone from its mouth. Then he watered Laban's sheep. Now Laban was the brother of Rebekah, Jacob's mother. ¹¹Then Jacob kissed Rachel and cried. ¹²He told her that he was from her father's family. . . . So Rachel ran home and told her father.

¹³ᵃWhen Laban heard the news about his sister's son Jacob, Laban ran to meet him. Laban hugged him and kissed him and brought him to his house. ¹⁴Then Laban said, "You are my own flesh and blood."

So Jacob stayed there a month. ¹⁵Then Laban said to Jacob, "You are my relative. But it is not right for you to keep on working for me without pay. What would you like me to pay you?"

¹⁶Now Laban had two daughters. The older was Leah, and the younger was Rachel. ¹⁷Leah had weak eyes, but Rachel was very beautiful. ¹⁸Jacob loved Rachel. So he said to Laban, "Let me marry

your younger daughter Rachel. If you will, I will work seven years for you."

¹⁹Laban said, "It would be better for her to marry you than someone else. So stay here with me." ²⁰So Jacob worked for Laban seven years so he could marry Rachel. But they seemed to him like just a few days. This was because he loved Rachel very much.

²¹After seven years Jacob said to Laban, "Give me Rachel so that I may marry her. The time I promised to work for you is over."

²²So Laban gave a feast for all the people there.

[23a]That evening Laban brought his daughter Leah to Jacob. [25b]In the morning . . . he said to Laban, "What have you done to me? I worked hard for you so that I could marry Rachel! Why did you trick me?"

[26]Laban said, "In our country we do not allow the younger daughter to marry before the older daughter. [27]But complete the full week of the marriage ceremony with Leah. I will give you Rachel to marry also. But you must serve me another seven years."

[28]So Jacob did this and completed the week with Leah. Then Laban gave him his daughter Rachel as a wife.

Jacob Wrestles with God

(From Genesis 32 and 33)

32:[3]Jacob's brother Esau was living in the area called Seir in the country of Edom. Jacob sent messengers to Esau. [4]Jacob told the messengers, "Give this message to my master Esau: 'This is what Jacob, your servant, says: I have lived with Laban and have remained there until now. [5]I have cattle, donkeys, flocks, and male and female servants. I send this message to you and ask you to accept us.'"

[6]The messengers returned to Jacob and said, "We went to your brother Esau. He is coming to meet you. And he has 400 men with him."

[7a]Then Jacob was very afraid and worried.

⁹Jacob said, "God of my father Abraham! God of my father Isaac! Lord, you told me to return to my country and my family. You said that you would do good to me. ¹⁰ᵃI am not worthy of the kindness and continual goodness you have shown me. ¹¹Please save me from my brother Esau. I am afraid he will come and kill all of us, even the mothers with the children."

²²⁻²³During the night Jacob rose and . . . sent his family and everything he had across the river. ²⁴But Jacob stayed behind alone. And a man came and wrestled with him until the sun came up. ²⁵The man saw he could not defeat Jacob. So he struck Jacob's hip and put it out of joint. ²⁶Then the man said to Jacob, "Let me go. The sun is coming up."

But Jacob said, "I will let you go if you will bless me."

²⁷The man said to him, "What is your name?"

And he answered, "Jacob."

²⁸Then the man said, "Your name will no longer be Jacob. Your name will now be Israel, because you have wrestled with God and with men. And you have won." ²⁹ᵇThen he blessed Jacob there.

³⁰So Jacob named that place Peniel. He said, "I have seen God face to face. But my life was saved." ³¹Then the sun rose as he was leaving that place. Jacob was limping because of his leg. ³²So even today the people of Israel do not eat the muscle

that is on the hip joint of animals. This is because Jacob was touched there.

33:¹ᵃJacob looked up and saw Esau coming. With him were 400 men. ³Jacob . . . bowed down flat on the ground seven times as he was walking toward his brother. ⁴But Esau ran to meet Jacob. Esau put his arms around him and hugged him. Then Esau kissed him, and they both cried.

Joseph and His Brothers

(From Genesis 35 and 37)

35:²²ᵇJacob had 12 sons. ²³He had 6 sons by his wife Leah. Reuben was his first son. Then Leah had Simeon, Levi, Judah, Issachar and Zebulun.

²⁴He had 2 sons by his wife Rachel: Joseph and Benjamin.
²⁵He had 2 sons by Rachel's slave girl Bilhah: Dan and Naphtali.
²⁶ᵃAnd he had 2 sons by Leah's slave girl Zilpah: Gad and Asher.
37:¹Jacob lived in the land of Canaan, where his father had lived. ²This is the family history of Jacob.

Joseph was a young man, 17 years old. He and his brothers cared for the flocks. . . . Joseph gave his father bad reports about his brothers. ³Joseph was born when his father Israel, also called Jacob, was old. So Israel loved Joseph more than his other sons. He made Joseph a special robe with long sleeves. ⁴Joseph's brothers saw that their father loved Joseph more than he loved them. So they hated their brother and could not speak to him politely.

⁵One time Joseph had a dream. When he told his brothers about it, they hated him even more. ⁶Joseph said, "Listen to the dream I had. ⁷We were in the field tying bundles of wheat together. My bundle stood up, and your bundles of wheat gathered around mine. Your bundles bowed down to mine."

⁸His brothers said, "Do you really think you will be king over us? Do you truly think you will rule over us?" His brothers hated him even more now. They hated him because of his dreams and what he had said.

⁹Then Joseph had another dream. He told his brothers about it also. He said "Listen, I had another dream. I saw the sun, moon and 11 stars bowing down to me."

¹⁰Joseph also told his father about this dream. But his father scolded him, saying, "What kind of dream is this? Do you really believe that your mother, your brothers and I will bow down to you?" ¹¹Joseph's brothers were jealous of him. But his father thought about what all these things could mean.

¹²One day Joseph's brothers went to Shechem to herd their father's sheep. ¹³Jacob said to Joseph, "Go to Shechem. Your brothers are there herding the sheep."

Joseph answered, "I will go."

¹⁴His father said, "Go and see if your brothers and the sheep are all right. Then come back and tell me." So Joseph's father sent him from the Valley of Hebron.

When Joseph came to Shechem, ¹⁵a man found him wandering in the field. He asked Joseph, "What are you looking for?"

¹⁶ªJoseph answered, "I am looking for my brothers. Can you tell me where they are herding the sheep?"

¹⁷The man said, "They have already gone. I heard them say they were going to Dothan." So Joseph went to look for his brothers and found them in Dothan.

Joseph Sold into Slavery
(From Genesis 37)

37:¹⁸Joseph's brothers saw him coming from far away. Before he reached them, they made a plan to kill him. ¹⁹They said to each other, "Here comes that dreamer. ²⁰Let's kill him and throw his body into one of the wells. We can tell our father that a wild animal killed him. Then we will see what will become of his dreams."

²¹But Reuben heard their plan and saved Joseph. He said, "Let's not kill him. ²²Don't spill any blood. Throw him into this well here in the desert. But don't hurt him!" Reuben planned to save Joseph later and send him back to his father. ²³So when Joseph came to his brothers, they pulled off his

robe with long sleeves. ²⁴Then they threw him into the well. It was empty. There was no water in it.

²⁵While Joseph was in the well, the brothers sat down to eat. When they looked up, they saw a group of Ishmaelites. They were traveling from Gilead to Egypt. Their camels were carrying spices, balm and myrrh.

²⁶Then Judah said to his brothers, "What will we gain if we kill our brother and hide his death? ²⁷Let's sell him to these Ishmaelites. Then we will not be guilty of killing our own brother. . . . " And the other brothers agreed. ²⁸So when the Midianite traders came by, the brothers took Joseph out of the well. They sold him to the Ishmaelites for eight ounces of silver. And the Ishmaelites took him to Egypt.

²⁹Reuben was not with his brothers when they sold Joseph to the Ishmaelites. When Reuben came back to the well, Joseph was not there. Reuben tore his clothes to show he was sad. ³⁰Then he went back to his brothers and said, "The boy is not there! What will I do?" ³¹The brothers killed a goat and dipped Joseph's long-sleeved robe in its blood. ³²Then they brought the robe to their father. They said, "We found this robe. Look it over carefully. See if it is your son's robe."

³³Jacob looked it over and said, "It is my son's robe! Some savage animal has eaten him. My son

Joseph has been torn to pieces!" ³⁴Then Jacob tore his clothes and put on rough cloth to show that he was sad. He continued to be sad about his son for a long time. ³⁵All of Jacob's sons and daughters tried to comfort him. But he could not be comforted. Jacob said, "I will be sad about my son until the day I die." So Jacob cried for his son Joseph.

³⁶Meanwhile the Midianites who had bought Joseph had taken him to Egypt. There they sold him to Potiphar. Potiphar was an officer to the king of Egypt and captain of the palace guard.

Joseph Thrown into Prison

(From Genesis 39)

39:²The Lord was with Joseph, and he became a successful man. He lived in the house of his master, Potiphar the Egyptian.

³Potiphar saw that the Lord was with Joseph. He saw that the Lord made Joseph successful in everything he did. ⁴So Potiphar was very happy with Joseph. He allowed Joseph to be his personal servant. He put Joseph in charge of the house. Joseph was trusted with everything Potiphar owned. ⁵ᵇThen the Lord blessed the people in Potiphar's house because of Joseph. And the Lord blessed everything that belonged to Potiphar, both in the house and in the field.

⁶ᵇNow Joseph was well built and handsome. ⁷ᵃAfter some time the wife of Joseph's master began to desire Joseph.

[8]But Joseph refused. He said to her, "My master trusts me with everything in his house. He has put me in charge of everything he owns. [9]There is no one in his house greater than I. He has not kept anything from me, except you. And that is because you are his wife. How can I do such an evil thing? It is a sin against God."

[10]The woman talked to Joseph every day, but he refused to . . . even spend time with her.

[11]One day Joseph went into the house to do his work as usual. He was the only man in the house at that time. [12]His master's wife grabbed his coat. She said to him, "Come . . . with me." But Joseph left his coat in her hand and ran out of the house.

[13]She saw what Joseph had done. He had left his coat in her hands and had run outside. [14a]So she called to the servants in her house. She said, "Look! This Hebrew slave was brought here to shame us." [16]She kept his coat until her husband came home. [17]And she told her husband the same story. She said, "This Hebrew slave you brought here came in to shame me! [18]When he came near me, I screamed. He ran away, but he left his coat."

¹⁹When Joseph's master heard what his wife said Joseph had done, he became very angry. ²⁰So Potiphar arrested Joseph and put him into prison. This prison was where the king's prisoners were put. And Joseph stayed there in the prison. ²¹But the Lord was with Joseph and showed him kindness. The Lord caused the prison warden to like Joseph. ²²The prison warden chose Joseph to take care of all the prisoners. He was responsible for whatever was done in the prison. ²³The warden paid no attention to anything that was in Joseph's care. This was because the Lord was with Joseph. The Lord made Joseph successful in everything he did.

Joseph Interprets the King's Dream

(From Genesis 41)

41:¹Two years later the king had a dream. He dreamed he was standing on the bank of the Nile River. ²He saw seven fat and beautiful cows come up out of the river. They stood there, eating the grass. ³Then seven more cows came up out of the river. But they were thin and ugly. They stood beside the seven beautiful cows on the bank of the Nile. ⁴The seven thin and ugly cows ate the seven beautiful fat cows. Then the king woke up. ⁵The king slept again and dreamed a second time. In his dream he saw seven full and good heads of grain growing on one stalk. ⁶After that, seven more heads of grain sprang up. But they were thin and burned by the hot east wind. ⁷The thin heads of grain ate the seven full and good heads. Then the king woke up again. And he realized it was only a dream. ⁸The next morning the king was troubled about these dreams. So he sent for all the magicians and wise men of Egypt. The king told them his dreams. But no one could explain their meaning to him.

⁹Then the chief officer who served wine to the king said to him, "I remember something I promised to do. But I had forgotten about it. ¹⁰There was a time when you were angry with me and the baker. You put us in prison in the house of the captain of the guard. ¹¹In prison we each had a dream on the same night. Each dream had a different meaning. ¹²A young Hebrew man was in the prison with us. . . . We told him our dreams, and he explained their meanings to us. He told each man the meaning of his dream."

¹⁴So the king called for Joseph. The guards quickly brought him out of the prison. He shaved, put on clean clothes and went before the king.

¹⁵The king said to Joseph, "I have had a dream. But no one can explain its meaning to me. I have heard that you can explain a dream when someone tells it to you."

¹⁶Joseph answered the king, "I am not able to explain the meaning of dreams. God will do this for the king.

²⁹"You will have seven years of good crops and plenty to eat in all the land of Egypt. ³⁰But after those seven years, there will come seven years of

hunger. All the food that grew in the land of Egypt will be forgotten. The time of hunger will eat up the land. ³¹People will forget what it was like to have plenty of food. This is because the hunger that follows will be so great. ³²You had two dreams which mean the same thing. This shows that God has firmly decided that this will happen. And he will make it happen soon."

³⁹So the king said to Joseph, "God has shown you all this. There is no one as wise and understanding as you are. ⁴⁰I will put you in charge of my palace. All the people will obey your orders. Only I will be greater than you."

The Dreams Come True

(From Genesis 41, 42, 45, and 46)

41:⁵³The seven years of good crops came to an end in the land of Egypt. ⁵⁴Then the seven years of hunger began, just as Joseph had said. In all the lands people had nothing to eat. But in Egypt there was food. ⁵⁵The time of hunger became terrible in all of Egypt. The people cried to the king for food. He said to all the Egyptians, "Go to Joseph. Do whatever he tells you to do."

[56a]The hunger was everywhere in that part of the world. And Joseph opened the storehouses and sold grain to the people of Egypt. [57a]And all the people in that part of the world came to Joseph in Egypt to buy grain.

42:[1]Jacob learned that there was grain in Egypt. So he said to his sons, "Why are you just sitting here looking at one another? [2]I have heard that there is grain in Egypt. Go down there and buy grain for us to eat. Then we will live and not die."

[3]So ten of Joseph's brothers went down to buy grain from Egypt. [4]But Jacob did not send Benjamin, Joseph's brother, with them. Jacob was afraid that something terrible might happen to Benjamin.

[6]Now Joseph was governor over Egypt. He was the one who sold the grain to people who came to buy it. So Joseph's brothers came to him. They bowed facedown on the ground before him. [7]When Joseph saw his brothers, he knew who they were. But he acted as if he didn't know them. He asked unkindly, "Where do you come from?"

They answered, "We have come from the land of Canaan to buy food."

[8]Joseph knew they were his brothers. But they did not know who he was. [9]And Joseph remem-

bered his dreams about his brothers bowing down to him.

45:³ He said to his brothers, "I am Joseph. Is my father still alive?" But the brothers could not answer him, because they were very afraid of him.

⁴So Joseph said to them, "Come close to me." So the brothers came close to him. And he said to them, "I am your brother Joseph. You sold me as a slave to go to Egypt. ⁵Now don't be worried. Don't be angry with yourselves because you sold me here. God sent me here ahead of you to save peoples' lives.

⁹"So leave quickly and go to my father. Tell him, 'Your son Joseph says: God has made me master over all Egypt. Come down to me quickly. ¹⁰Live in the land of Goshen. You will be near me. Also your children, your grandchildren, your flocks and herds and all that you have will be near me. ¹¹I will care for you during the next five years of hunger. In this way, you and your family and all that you have will not starve.'"

46:⁶ᵇ So Jacob went to Egypt with all his descendants. ⁷He took his sons and grandsons, his daughters and granddaughters. He took all his family to Egypt with him.

Trouble for the People of Israel

(From Exodus 1)

1:¹ When Jacob, also called Israel, went to Egypt, he took his sons. And each son took his own family

41

with him. These are the names of the sons of Israel: ²Reuben, Simeon, Levi, Judah, ³Issachar, Zebulun, Benjamin, ⁴Dan, Naphtali, Gad and Asher. ⁵There was a total of 70 people who were descendants of Jacob. Jacob's son Joseph was already in Egypt.

⁶By some time later, Joseph and his brothers had died, along with all the people who had lived at that same time. ⁷But the people of Israel had many children, and their number grew greatly. They became very strong, and the country of Egypt was filled with them.

⁸Then a new king began to rule Egypt. He did not know who Joseph was. ⁹This king said to his people, "Look! The people of Israel are too many! And they are too strong for us to handle! ¹⁰We must make plans against them. If we don't, the number of their people will grow even more. Then if there is a war, they might join our enemies. Then they could fight us and escape from the country!"

¹¹So the Egyptians made life hard for the people of Israel. They put slave masters over the Israelites. The slave masters forced the Israelites to build the cities Pithom and Rameses for the king. These cities were supply centers in which the Egyptians stored things. ¹²The Egyptians forced the Israelites to work even harder. But this made the Israelites grow in number and spread more. So the Egyptians became more afraid of them. ¹³They forced the Israelites to work even harder. ¹⁴The Egyptians made life hard for the Israelites. They forced the Israelites to work

very hard making bricks and mortar. They also forced them to do all kinds of hard work in the fields. The Egyptians were not merciful to 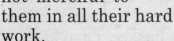 them in all their hard work.

¹⁵There were two Hebrew nurses named Shiphrah and Puah. These nurses helped the Israelite women give birth to their babies. The king of Egypt said to the nurses, ¹⁶"When you are helping the Hebrew women give birth to their babies, watch! If the baby is a girl, let the baby live. But if it is a boy, kill it!" ¹⁷But the nurses feared God. So they did not do as the king told them. They let all the boy babies live. ¹⁸Then the king of Egypt sent for the nurses. He said, "Why did you do this? Why did you let the boys live?"

¹⁹The nurses said to him, "The Hebrew women are much stronger than the Egyptian women. They give birth to their babies before we can get there." ²⁰God was good to the nurses. And the Hebrew people continued to grow in number. So they became even stronger. ²¹Because the nurses feared God, he gave them families of their own.

²²So the king commanded all his people: "Every time a boy is born to the Hebrews, you must throw him into the Nile River. But let all the girl babies live."

Baby in a Basket

(From Exodus 2)

2:¹There was a man from the family of Levi. He married a woman who was also from the family of Levi. ²She became pregnant and gave birth to a son. She saw how wonderful the baby was, and she hid him for three months. ³But after three months, she was not able to hide the baby any longer. So she got a basket and covered it with tar so that it would float. She put the baby in the basket. Then she put the basket among the tall grass at the edge of the Nile River. ⁴The baby's sister stood a short distance away. She wanted to see what would happen to him.

⁵Then the daughter of the king of Egypt came to the river. She was going to take a bath. Her servant girls were walking beside the river. She saw the basket in the tall grass. So she sent her slave girl to get it. ⁶The king's daughter opened the basket and saw the baby boy. He was crying, and she felt sorry for him. She said, "This is one of the Hebrew babies."

⁷Then the baby's sister asked the king's daughter, "Would you like me to find a Hebrew woman to nurse the baby for you?"

⁸The king's daughter said, "Yes, please." So the girl went and got the baby's own mother.

⁹The king's daughter said to the woman, "Take this baby and nurse him for me. I will pay you." So the woman took her baby and nursed him. ¹⁰After the child had grown older, the woman took him to the king's daughter. She adopted the baby as her own son. The king's daughter named him Moses, because she had pulled him out of the water.

¹¹Moses grew and became a man. One day he visited his people, the Hebrews. He saw that they were forced to work very hard. He saw an Egyptian beating a Hebrew man, one of Moses' own people. ¹²Moses looked all around and saw that no one was watching. So he killed the Egyptian and hid his body in the sand.

¹³The next day Moses returned and saw two Hebrew men fighting each other. He saw that one man was in the wrong. Moses said to that man, "Why are you hitting one of your own people?"

¹⁴The man answered, "Who made you our ruler and judge? Are you going to kill me as you killed the Egyptian?"

Then Moses was afraid. He thought, "Now everyone knows what I did."

¹⁵When the king heard about what Moses had done, he tried to kill Moses. But Moses ran away from the king and went to live in the land of Midian. There he sat down near a well.

The Burning Bush

(From Exodus 2 and 3)

2:¹⁶ᵃThere was a priest in Midian who had seven daughters. His daughters went to [the well where

Moses was sitting] to get water for their father's sheep. [17]But some shepherds came and chased the girls away. Then Moses defended the girls and watered their sheep.

[18]Then they went back to their father Reuel, also called Jethro. He asked them, "Why have you come home early today?"

[19]The girls answered, "The shepherds chased us away. But an Egyptian defended us. He got water for us and watered our sheep."

[20]He asked his daughters, "Where is this man? Why did you leave him? Invite him to eat with us."

[21]Moses agreed to stay with Jethro. And he gave his daughter Zipporah to Moses to be his wife. [22]Zipporah gave birth to a son, and Moses named him Gershom. Moses named him this because Moses was a stranger in a land that was not his own.

[23]After a long time, the king of Egypt died. The people of Israel groaned because they were forced to work very hard. They cried for help. And God heard them. [24]God heard their cries, and he remembered the agreement he had made with Abraham, Isaac and Jacob. [25]God saw the troubles of the people of Israel, and he was concerned about them.

3:[1]One day Moses was taking care of Jethro's sheep. Jethro was the priest of Midian and also Moses' father-in-law. Moses led the sheep to the west side of the desert. He came to Sinai, the mountain of God. [2]There the angel of the Lord appeared to Moses in flames of fire coming out of a bush. Moses saw that the bush was on fire, but it was not burning up. ³So Moses said, "I will go closer to this strange thing. How can a bush continue burning without burning up?"

⁴The Lord saw Moses was coming to look at the bush. So God called to him from the bush, "Moses, Moses!"

And Moses said, "Here I am."

⁵Then God said, "Do not come any closer. Take off your sandals. You are standing on holy ground. ⁶I am the God of your ancestors. I am the God of Abraham, the God of Isaac and the God of Jacob." Moses covered his face because he was afraid to look at God.

⁷The Lord said, "I have seen the troubles my people have suffered in Egypt. And I have heard their cries when the Egyptian slave masters hurt them. I am concerned about their pain. ⁸ᵃI have come down to save them from the Egyptians. I will bring them out of that land. I will lead them to a good land with lots of room. This is a land where much food grows. ¹⁰So now I am sending you to the king of Egypt. Go! Bring my people, the Israelites, out of Egypt!"

"Let My People Go!"

(From Exodus 7 and 12)

7:¹⁴Then the Lord said to Moses, "The king is being stubborn. He refuses to let the people go.

[15a]In the morning the king will go out to the Nile River. Go meet him by the edge of the river. [16]Tell him this: The Lord, the God of the Hebrews, sent me to you. He said, 'Let my people go worship me in the desert.' Until now you have not listened. [17]This is what the Lord says: 'This is how you will know that I am the Lord. I will strike the water of the Nile River with this stick in my hand. And the water will change into blood. [18]Then the fish in the Nile will die, and the river will begin to stink. And the Egyptians will not be able to drink the water from the Nile.'"

[19]The Lord said to Moses, "Tell Aaron to stretch the walking stick in his hand over the rivers, canals, ponds and pools in Egypt. The water will become blood everywhere in Egypt. There even will be blood in the wooden buckets and stone jars."

[20]So Moses and Aaron did just as the Lord had commanded. Aaron raised his walking stick and struck the water in the Nile River. He did this in front of the king and his officers. So all the water in the Nile changed into blood. [21]The fish in the Nile died, and the river began to stink. So the Egyptians could not drink water from it. Blood was everywhere in the land of Egypt.

12:[21]Then Moses called all the older leaders of Israel together. He told them, "Get the animals for your families. Kill the animals for the Passover. [22]Take a branch of the hyssop plant and dip it into the bowl filled with blood. Wipe the blood on the sides and tops of the doorframes. No one may leave

his house until morning. ²³The Lord will go through Egypt to kill the Egyptians. He will see the blood on the sides and tops of the doorframes. Then the Lord will pass over that house. He will not let the one who brings death come into your houses and kill you.

²⁴"You must keep this command. This law is for you and your descendants from now on. ²⁵Do this when you go to the land the Lord has promised to give to you. ²⁶When your children ask you, 'Why are we doing these things?' ²⁷you will say, 'This is the Passover sacrifice to honor the Lord. When we

were in Egypt, the Lord passed over the houses of Israel. The Lord killed the Egyptians, but he saved our homes.'" So now the people bowed down and worshiped the Lord. [28]They did just as the Lord commanded Moses and Aaron.

[29]At midnight the Lord killed all the firstborn sons in the land of Egypt. The firstborn of the king, who sat on the throne, died. Even the firstborn of the prisoner in jail died. Also all the firstborn farm animals died. [30]The king, his officers and all the Egyptians got up during the night. Someone had died in every house. So there was loud crying everywhere in Egypt.

[31]During the night the king called for Moses and Aaron. He said to them, "Get up and leave my people. You and your people may do as you have asked. Go and worship the Lord. [32]Take all of your sheep and cattle as you have asked. Go. And also bless me." [33]The Egyptians also asked the Israelites to hurry and leave. They said, "If you don't leave, we will all die!"

Walls of Water

(From Exodus 14)

14:[5]The king of Egypt was told that the people of Israel had already left. Then he and his officers changed their minds about them. They said, "What have we done? We have let the people of Israel leave. We have lost our slaves!" [6]So the king prepared his war chariot and took his army with him.

⁷He took 600 of his best chariots. He also took all the other chariots of Egypt. Each chariot had an officer in it. ⁸The Lord made the king of Egypt stubborn. So he chased the Israelites, who were leaving victoriously. ⁹ᵇThey caught up with the Israelites while they were camped by the Red Sea. . . .

¹⁰The Israelites saw the king and his army coming after them. They were very frightened and cried to the Lord for help. ¹¹ᵃThey said to Moses, "What have you done to us? Why did you bring us out of Egypt to die in the desert?"

¹³But Moses answered, "Don't be afraid! Stand still and see the Lord save you today. You will never see these Egyptians again after today. ¹⁴You will only need to remain calm. The Lord will fight for you."

¹⁵Then the Lord said to Moses, "Why are you crying out to me? Command the people of Israel to start moving. ¹⁶Raise your walking stick and hold it over the sea. The sea will split. Then the people can cross the sea on dry land. ¹⁷I have made the Egyptians stubborn so they will chase the Israelites. But I will be honored when I defeat the king and all of his chariot drivers and chariots. ¹⁸I will defeat the king, his chariot drivers and chariots. Then Egypt will know that I am the Lord."

²¹Moses held his hand over the sea. All that night the Lord drove back the sea with a strong east wind. And so he made the sea become dry ground. The water was split. ²²And the Israelites went through the sea on dry land. A wall of water was on both sides.

²³Then all the king's horses, chariots and chariot drivers followed them into the sea. ²⁴Between two and six o'clock in the morning, the Lord looked down from the pillar of cloud and fire at the Egyptian army. He made them panic. ²⁵He kept the wheels of the chariots from turning. This made it hard to drive the chariots. The Egyptians shouted, "Let's get away from the Israelites! The Lord is fighting for them and against us Egyptians."

²⁶Then the Lord told Moses, "Hold your hand over the sea. Then the water will come back over the Egyptians, their chariots and chariot drivers." ²⁷So Moses raised his hand over the sea. And at dawn the water became deep again. The Egyptians were

trying to run from it. But the Lord swept them away into the sea.

²⁹But the people of Israel crossed the sea on dry land. There was a wall of water on their right and on their left.

Bread from Heaven

(From Exodus 16)

16:¹Then the whole Israelite community left Elim. They came to the Desert of Sin. This place was between Elim and Sinai. They came to this place on the fifteenth day of the second month after they had left Egypt. ²Then the whole Israelite community grumbled to Moses and Aaron in the desert. ³The Israelites said to them, "It would have been better if the Lord had killed us in the land of Egypt. There we had meat to eat. We had all the food we wanted. But you have brought us into this desert. You will starve us to death here."

⁴Then the Lord said to Moses, "I will cause food to fall like rain from the sky. This food will be for all of you. Every day the people must go out and gather what they need for that day. I will do this to see if the people will do what I teach them. ⁵On the sixth day of each week, they are to gather twice as much as they gather on other days. Then they are to prepare it."

⁶So Moses and Aaron said to all the Israelites: "This evening you will know that the Lord is the one who brought you out of Egypt. ⁷Tomorrow

morning you will see the greatness of the Lord. He has heard you grumble against him. We are nothing. You are not grumbling against us, but against the Lord." ⁸And Moses said, "Each evening the Lord will give you meat to eat. And every morning he will give you all the bread you want. He will do this because he has heard you grumble against him. You are not grumbling against Aaron and me. You are grumbling against the Lord."

⁹Then Moses said to Aaron, "Speak to the whole community of the Israelites. Say to them, 'Meet together in front of the Lord, because he has heard your grumblings.'"

¹⁰So Aaron spoke to the whole community of the Israelites. While he was speaking, they looked toward the desert. There the greatness of the Lord appeared in a cloud.

¹¹The Lord said to Moses, ¹²"I have heard the grumblings of the people of Israel. So tell them, 'At twilight you will eat meat. And every morning you

will eat all the bread you want. Then you will know I am the Lord, your God.'"

¹³That evening, quail came and covered the camp. And in the morning dew lay around the camp. ¹⁴When the dew was gone, thin flakes like frost were on the desert ground. ¹⁵When the Israelites saw it, they asked each other, "What is that?" They asked this question because they did not know what it was.

So Moses told them, "This is the bread the Lord has given you to eat. ¹⁶The Lord has commanded, 'Each one of you must gather what he needs. Gather about two quarts for every person in your family.'"

¹⁷So the people of Israel did this. Some people gathered much, and some gathered little.

God's Commands
and the People's Sin

(From Exodus 19, 20, 31, and 32)

19:¹Exactly three months after the Israelites had left Egypt, they reached the Desert of Sinai. ²They had left Rephidim and had come to the Desert of Sinai. The Israelites camped in the desert in front of Mount Sinai.

^{16b}There was thunder and lightning with a thick cloud on the mountain. And there was a very loud blast from a trumpet. All the people in the camp were frightened. ¹⁷Then Moses led the people out of the camp to meet God. They stood at the foot of the

mountain. ¹⁹ᵇThen Moses spoke, and the voice of God answered him.

20:¹Then God spoke all these words:

²"I am the Lord your God. I brought you out of the land of Egypt where you were slaves.

³"You must not have any other gods except me.

⁴"You must not make for yourselves any idols. Don't make something that looks like anything in the sky above or on the earth below or in the water below the land.

⁷"You must not use the name of the Lord your God thoughtlessly. The Lord will punish anyone who is guilty and misuses his name.

⁸"Remember to keep the Sabbath as a holy day.

¹²ᵃ"Honor your father and your mother. Then you will live a long·time in the land.

¹³"You must not murder anyone.

¹⁴"You must not be guilty of adultery.

¹⁵"You must not steal.

¹⁶"You must not tell lies about your neighbor in court.

¹⁷"You must not want to take your neighbor's house. . . . You must not want to take anything that belongs to your neighbor."

31:¹⁸So the Lord finished speaking to Moses on Mount Sinai. Then the Lord gave him the two stone tablets with the agreement written on them. The finger of God wrote the commands on the stones.

32:¹The people saw that a long time had passed. And Moses had not come down from the mountain. So they gathered around Aaron. They said to him,

"Moses led us out of Egypt. But we don't know what has happened to him. So make us gods who will lead us."

²ᵃAaron said to the people, "Take off the gold earrings that your wives, sons and daughters are wearing." ⁴ᵃAaron took the gold from the people. Then he melted it and made a statue of a calf.

⁷And the Lord said to Moses, "Go down from this mountain. Your people, the people you brought out of the land of Egypt, have done a terrible sin."

¹⁵ᵃThen Moses went down the mountain. In his hands he had the two stone tablets with the agreement on them.

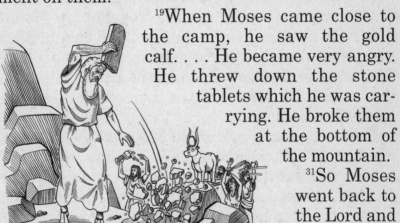

¹⁹When Moses came close to the camp, he saw the gold calf. . . . He became very angry. He threw down the stone tablets which he was carrying. He broke them at the bottom of the mountain.

³¹So Moses went back to the Lord and said, "How terrible it is! These people have sinned horribly! They have made for themselves gods from gold. ³²ᵃNow, forgive them of this sin."

Moses' Face Was Shining

(From Exodus 34)

34:¹The Lord said to Moses, "Cut two more stone tablets like the first two. I will write the same words on them that were on the first two stones which you broke. ²Be ready tomorrow morning. Then come up on Mount Sinai. Stand before me there on the top of the mountain. ³No one may come with you. No one should even be seen any place on the mountain. Not even the sheep or cattle may eat grass near that mountain."

⁴So Moses cut two stone tablets like the first ones. Then early the next morning he went up Mount Sinai. He did this just as the Lord had commanded him. Moses carried the two stone tablets with him. ⁵Then the Lord came down in the cloud and stood there with Moses. And the Lord called out his name, the Lord.

⁶The Lord passed in front of Moses and said, "I am the Lord. The Lord is a God who shows mercy and is kind. The Lord doesn't become angry quickly. The Lord has great love and faithfulness. ⁷ᵃThe Lord is kind to thousands of people. The Lord forgives people for wrong and sin and turning against him. But the Lord does not forget to punish guilty people."

⁸Then Moses quickly bowed to the ground and worshiped. ⁹Moses said, "Lord, if you are pleased with me, please go with us. I know that these are stubborn people. But forgive our evil and our sin. Take us as your own people."

¹⁰Then the Lord said, "I am making this agreement with you. I will do miracles in front of all

your people. These things have never before been done for any other nation on earth. The people with you will see my work. I, the Lord will do wonderful things for you."

²⁸Moses stayed there with the Lord 40 days and 40 nights. During that time he did not eat food or drink water. And Moses wrote the words of the agreement—the Ten Commandments—on the stone tablets.

²⁹Then Moses came down from Mount Sinai. In his hands he was carrying the two stone tablets of the agreement. But Moses did not know that his face was shining because he had talked with the Lord. ³⁰Aaron and all the people of Israel saw that Moses' face was shining. So they were afraid to go near him. ³¹But Moses called to them. So Aaron and all the leaders of the people returned to Moses. Moses talked with them. ³²After that, all the people of Israel came near him. And he gave them all the commands that the Lord had given him on Mount Sinai. ³³When Moses finished speaking to the people, he put a covering over his face. ³⁴Anytime Moses went before the Lord to speak with him, Moses took off the covering until he came out. Then Moses would come out and tell the people of Israel the things the Lord had commanded. ³⁵ᵃThe Israelites would see that Moses' face was shining. So he would cover his face again.

Twelve Spies

(From Numbers 13 and 14)

13:¹The Lord said to Moses, ²"Send men to explore the land of Canaan. I will give that land to the Israelites. Send one leader from each tribe."

³So Moses obeyed the Lord's command. He sent the Israelite leaders out from the Desert of Paran.

¹⁷Moses sent them to explore Canaan. He said, "Go through southern Canaan and then into the mountains. ¹⁸See what the land looks like. Are the people who live there strong or weak? Are there a few or many? ¹⁹What kind of land do they live in? Is it good or bad? What about the towns they live in— do they have walls, or are they open like camps? ²⁰What about the soil? Is it fertile or poor? Are there trees there? Try to bring back some of the fruit from that land." (It was the season for the first grapes.)

²¹So they went up and explored the land. They went from the Desert of Zin all the way to Rehob by Lebo Hamath. ²²ᵃThey went through the south-ern area to Hebron. ²³In the Valley of Eshcol, they cut off a branch of a grapevine. It had one bunch of grapes on it. They carried that branch on a

pole between two of them. They also got some pomegranates and figs. ²⁴They call that place the Valley of Eshcol. That is because the Israelites cut off the bunch of grapes there. ²⁵After 40 days of exploring the land, the men returned to the camp.

²⁶They came back to Moses and Aaron and all the Israelites at Kadesh. This was in the Desert of Paran. The men reported to them and showed everybody the fruit from the land. ²⁷They told Moses, "We went to the land where you sent us. It is a land where much food grows! Here is some of its fruit. ^{28a}But the people who live there are strong. Their cities are walled and large."

³⁰Then Caleb told the people near Moses to be quiet. Caleb said, "We should go up and take the land for ourselves. We can do it."

³¹But the men who had gone with him said, "We can't attack those people. They are stronger than we are." ³²And those men gave the Israelites a bad report about the land they explored. They said, "The land would eat us up. All the people we saw are very tall. ^{33b}We felt like grasshoppers. And we looked like grasshoppers to them."

14:²⁶ The Lord said to Moses and Aaron, ²⁷"How long will these evil people complain about me? I have heard these Israelites' grumbling and complaining. ²⁸So tell them, 'This is what the Lord says. I heard what you said. As surely as I live, I will do those things to you. ²⁹You will die in this desert. . . . You complained against me, the Lord. ³⁰Not one of you will enter and live in the land I promised to you. Only Caleb son of Jephunneh and Joshua son of Nun will go in.'"

The Bronze Snake

(From Numbers 21 and 22)

21:⁴The Israelites left Mount Hor and went on the road toward the Gulf of Aqaba. They did this to go around the country of Edom. But the people became impatient on the way. ⁵They grumbled at God and Moses. They said, "Why did you bring us out of Egypt? We will die in this desert! There is no bread! There is no water! And we hate this terrible food!"

⁶So the Lord sent them poisonous snakes. They bit the people, and many of the Israelites died. ⁷The people came to Moses and said, "We sinned when we grumbled at you and the Lord. Pray that the Lord will take away these snakes." So Moses prayed for the people.

⁸The Lord said to Moses, "Make a bronze snake. And put it on a pole. If anyone is bitten, he should look at it. Then he will live." ⁹So Moses made a bronze snake. And he put it on a pole. Then when a snake bit any-one, he looked at the bronze snake and lived.

22:¹Then the people of Israel went to the plains of Moab. They camped near the Jordan River across from Jericho.

³ᵃAnd Moab was scared of so many Israelites.

[4]The Moabites said to the older leaders of Midian, "This mob will take everything around us. It will be like an ox eating grass."

Balak son of Zippor was the king of Moab at this time. [5]He sent messengers to Balaam son of Beor at Pethor. . . . Balak said, "A nation has come out of Egypt. They cover the land. They have camped next to me. [6]They are too powerful for me. So come and put a curse on them. Maybe then I can defeat them and make them leave the area. I know that if you bless someone, the blessings happen. And if you put a curse on someone, it happens."

[7]The leaders of Moab and Midian went with payment in their hands. They found Balaam. Then they told him what Balak had said.

[12]But God said to Balaam, "Do not go with them. Don't put a curse on those people. I have blessed them."

[13]The next morning Balaam awoke and said to Balak's leaders, "Go back to your own country. The Lord will not let me go with you."

[14]So the Moabite leaders went back to Balak. They said, "Balaam refused to come with us."

[15]So Balak sent other leaders. He sent more leaders this time. And they were more important. [16]They went to Balaam and said, "Balak son of Zippor says this: Please don't let anything stop you from coming to me. [17b]Come and put a curse on these people for me."

[18]But Balaam answered Balak's servants, "King Balak could give me his palace full of silver and gold. But I cannot disobey the Lord my God in anything, great or small."

[20]That night God came to Balaam. He said, "These men have come to ask you to go with them. Go. But only do what I tell you."

Balaam's Donkey

(From Numbers 22 and 23)

22:[21]Balaam got up the next morning. He put a saddle on his donkey. Then he went with the Moabite leaders. [22]But God became angry because Balaam went. So the angel of the Lord stood in the road to stop Balaam. Balaam was riding his donkey. And he had two servants with him. [23]The donkey saw the angel of the Lord standing in the road. The angel had a sword in his hand. So the donkey left the road and went into the field. Balaam hit the donkey to force her back on the road.

[24]Later, the angel of the Lord stood on a narrow path between two vineyards. There were walls on both sides. [25]Again the donkey saw the angel of the Lord. So the donkey walked close to one wall. This crushed Balaam's foot against the wall. So he hit her again.

[26]The angel of the Lord went ahead again. The angel stood at a narrow place. It was too narrow to turn left or right. [27]The donkey saw the angel of the Lord. So she lay down under Balaam. Balaam was very angry and hit her

with his stick. ²⁸Then the Lord made the donkey talk. She said to Balaam, "What have I done to make you hit me three times?"

²⁹Balaam answered the donkey, "You have made me look foolish! I wish I had a sword in my hand! I would kill you right now!"

³⁰But the donkey said to Balaam, "I am your very own donkey. You have ridden me for years. Have I ever done this to you before?"

"No," Balaam said.

³¹Then the Lord let Balaam see the angel. The angel of the Lord was standing in the road with his sword drawn. Then Balaam bowed facedown on the ground.

³²The angel of the Lord asked Balaam, "Why have you hit your donkey three times? I have stood here to stop you. What you are doing is wrong. ³³The donkey saw me. She turned away from me three times. If she had not turned away, I would have killed you by now. But I would let her live."

³⁴Then Balaam said to the angel of the Lord, "I have sinned. I did not know you were standing in the road to stop me. If I am wrong, I will go back."

³⁵The angel of the Lord said to Balaam, "Go with these men. But say only what I tell you." So Balaam went with Balak's leaders.

23:^{16a}So the Lord came to Balaam. He told Balaam what to say.

¹⁷So Balaam went to Balak. . . . Balak asked him, "What did the Lord say?"

¹⁸Then Balaam gave this message:

"Stand up, Balak, and listen.
    Hear me, son of Zippor.

²⁰[God] told me to bless them.
   So I cannot change the blessing.
²¹He has found no wrong in the people of Jacob.
   He saw no fault in Israel.
The Lord their God is with them.
   They praise their King."

Joshua Becomes the Leader
of God's People

(From Deuteronomy 34 and Joshua 1)

34:¹Then Moses climbed up Mount Nebo. He went from the plains of Moab to the top of Mount Pisgah. It is across from Jericho. From there the Lord showed him all the land. He could see from Gilead to Dan. ²He could see all of Naphtali and the lands of Ephraim and Manasseh. He could see all the land of Judah as far as the Mediterranean Sea. ³He could see the southern desert and the whole Valley of Jericho up to Zoar. Jericho is called the city of palm trees. ⁴Then the Lord said to Moses, "This is the land I promised to Abraham, Isaac and Jacob. I said to them, 'I will give this land to your descendants.' I have let you look at it, Moses. But you will not cross over there."

⁵Then Moses, the servant of the Lord, died there in Moab. It was as the Lord had said. ⁶The Lord buried Moses in Moab in the valley opposite Beth Peor. But even today no one knows where his grave is. ⁷Moses was 120 years old when he died. His eyes were not weak. And he was still strong. ⁸The

Israelites cried for Moses for 30 days. They stayed in the plains of Moab until the time of sadness was over.

⁹Joshua son of Nun was then filled with wisdom. Moses had put his hands on Joshua. So the Israelites listened to Joshua. And they did what the Lord had commanded Moses.

JOSHUA

1:¹ᵇAfter Moses died, the Lord said to Joshua: ²"My servant Moses is dead. Now you and all these people go across the Jordan River. Go into the land I am giving to the people of Israel. ³I promised Moses I would give you this land. So I will give you every place you go in the land. ⁴ᵃAll the land from the desert in the south to Lebanon in the north will be yours. All the land from the great river, the Euphrates, in the east, to the Mediterranean Sea in the west will be yours. ⁵Just as I was with Moses, so I will be with you. No one will be able to stop you all your life. I will not leave you. I will never leave you alone.

⁶"Joshua, be strong and brave! You must lead these people so they can take their land. This is the land I promised their fathers I would give them. ⁷Be strong and brave. Be sure to obey all the teachings my servant Moses gave you. If you follow them exactly, you will be successful in everything you do. ⁸Always remember what is written in the

Book of the Teachings. Study it day and night. Then you will be sure to obey everything that is written there. If you do this, you will be wise and successful in everything. [9]Remember that I commanded you to be strong and brave. So don't be afraid. The Lord your God will be with you everywhere you go."

Rahab Hides the Spies

(From Joshua 2)

2:[1]Joshua son of Nun secretly sent out two spies from Acacia. Joshua said to them, "Go and look at the land. Look closely at the city of Jericho."

So the men went to Jericho. They went to the house of a [woman] and stayed there. This woman's name was Rahab.

[2]Someone told the king of Jericho, "Some men from Israel have come here tonight. They are spying out the land."

[3]So the king of Jericho sent this message to Rahab: "Bring out the men who came to you and entered your house. They have come to spy out our whole land."

[4]Now the woman had hidden the two men. She

said, "They did come here. But I didn't know where they came from. ⁵In the evening, when it was time to close the city gate, they left. I don't know where they went. Go quickly. Maybe you can catch them." ⁶(But the woman had taken the men up to the roof. She had hidden them there under stalks of flax. She had spread the flax out there to dry.) ⁷ªSo the king's men went out looking for the spies from Israel.

⁸The spies were ready to sleep for the night. So Rahab went to the roof and talked to them. ⁹She said, "I know the Lord has given this land to your people. You frighten us very much. Everyone living in this land is terribly afraid of you. ¹⁰ªWe are afraid because we have heard how the Lord helped you. We heard how he dried up the Red Sea when you came out of Egypt. ¹¹When we heard this, we became very frightened. Now our men are afraid to fight you. This is because the Lord your God rules the heavens above and the earth below! ¹²So now, make me a promise before the Lord. Promise that you will show kindness to my family just as I showed you kindness. Give me some proof that you will do this. ¹³Promise me you will allow my family to live. Save my father, mother, brothers, sisters and all of their families from death."

¹⁴The men agreed. They said, "We will trade our lives for your lives. Don't tell anyone what we are doing. When the Lord gives us our land, we will be kind to you. You may trust us."

¹⁵The house Rahab lived in was built on the city wall. So she used a rope to let the men down through a window. ¹⁶She said to them, "Go into the

hills. The king's men will not find you there. Hide there for three days. After the king's men return, you may go on your way."

¹⁷ᵃThe men said to her, "You must do as we say. ¹⁸You are using a red rope to help us escape. When we return to this land, you must tie it in the window through which you let us down. Bring your father, mother, brothers and all your family into your house. ¹⁹ᵃWe can keep everyone safe who stays in this house."

²¹Rahab answered, "I agree to this." So she sent them away, and they left. Then she tied the red rope in the window.

The People of Israel Cross the Jordan River

(From Joshua 3 and 4)

3:⁵Then Joshua told the people, "Make yourselves holy for the Lord. Tomorrow the Lord will do amazing things among you."

⁶Joshua said to the priests, "Take the Box of the Agreement. Cross over the river ahead of the people." So the priests lifted the Holy Box and carried it ahead of the people.

⁷Then the Lord said to Joshua, "Today I will begin to make you a great man to all the Israelites. So the people will know I am with you just as I was with Moses. ⁸The priests will carry the Box of the Agreement. Tell them this: 'Go to the edge of the Jordan River and stand in the water.'"

⁹Then Joshua said to the people of Israel, "Come here. Listen to the words of the Lord your God. ¹⁰ᵃHere is proof that the living God is with you. ¹¹ᵇThe Box of the Agreement will go ahead of you into the Jordan River. It is the Agreement with the Lord of the whole world. ¹³The priests will carry the Holy Box of the Lord, the Master of the whole world. They will carry it into the Jordan ahead of you. When they enter the water, the river will stop flowing. The water will be stopped. It will stand up in a heap as if a dam were there."

¹⁴So the priests carried the Box of the Agreement. And the people left the place where they had camped. Then they started across the Jordan River. ¹⁵During harvest the Jordan is flooded. So the river was at its fullest. The priests who were carrying the Holy Box came to the edge of the river. And they stepped into the water. ¹⁶Just at that moment, the water stopped flowing. It stood up in a heap a great distance away. . . . So the people crossed the river near Jericho. ¹⁷The ground there became dry. The priests carried the Box of the

Agreement with the Lord to the middle of the river and stopped. They waited there while all the people of Israel walked across. They crossed the Jordan River on dry land.

4:¹All the people finished crossing the Jordan.

Then the Lord said to Joshua, [2]"Choose 12 men from among the people. Choose 1 from each tribe. [3]Tell the men to get 12 large rocks from the middle of the river. Take them from where the priests stood. Carry the rocks and put them down where you stay tonight."

[8a]So the Israelites obeyed Joshua.

[21]Then [Joshua] spoke to the Israelites. He said, "In the future your children will ask you, 'What do these rocks mean?' [22]Tell them, 'Israel crossed the Jordan River on dry land. [23a]The Lord your God caused the water to stop flowing. The river was dry until the people finished crossing it. The Lord did the same thing for us at the Jordan that he did for the people at the Red Sea.'"

The Fall of Jericho

(From Joshua 6)

6:[1]Now the people of Jericho were afraid because the Israelites were near. So they closed the city gates and guarded them. No one went into the city. And no one came out.

[2]Then the Lord spoke to Joshua. He said, "Look, I have given you Jericho, its king and all its fighting men. [3]March around the city with your army one time every day. Do this for six days. [4]Have seven priests carry trumpets made from horns of male sheep. Tell them to march in front of the Holy Box. On the seventh day march around the city seven

times. On that day tell the priests to blow the trumpets as they march. ⁵They will make one long blast on the trumpets. When you hear that sound, have all the people give a loud shout. Then the walls of the city will fall. And the people will go straight into the city."

⁶So Joshua son of Nun called the priests together. He said to them, "Carry the Box of the Agreement with the Lord. Tell seven priests to carry trumpets and march in front of it." ⁷Then Joshua ordered the people, "Now go! March around the city. The soldiers with weapons should march in front of the Box of the Agreement with the Lord."

⁸So Joshua finished speaking to the people. Then the seven priests began marching before the Lord. They carried the seven trumpets and blew them as they marched. The priests carrying the Box of the Agreement with the Lord followed them. ⁹The soldiers with weapons marched in front of the priests. And armed men walked behind the Holy Box. They were blowing their trumpets. ¹⁰But Joshua had told the people not to give a war cry. He said, "Don't shout. Don't say a word until the day I tell you. Then shout!" ¹¹So Joshua had the Holy Box of the Lord carried around the city one time. Then they went back to camp for the night.

¹²Early the next morning Joshua got up. And the priests carried the Holy Box of the Lord again. ¹⁴So on the second day they marched around the city one time. Then they went back to camp. They did this every day for six days.

¹⁵ᵃOn the seventh day they got up at dawn. They marched around the city seven times. ¹⁶The seventh

time around the priests blew their trumpets. Then Joshua gave the command: "Now, shout! The Lord has given you this city! [17]The city and everything in it are to be destroyed as an offering to the Lord. Only Rahab . . . and everyone in her house should remain alive. They must not be killed. This is because Rahab hid the two spies we sent out."

[20]When the priests blew the trumpets, the people shouted. At the sound of the trumpets and the people's shout, the walls fell. And everyone ran straight into the city. So the Israelites defeated that city.

The Longest Day

(From Joshua 10)

10:[1]At this time Adoni-Zedek was the king of Jerusalem. He heard that Joshua had defeated Ai and completely destroyed it. He learned that Joshua had done the same thing to Jericho and its king. The king also learned that the Gibeonites had made a peace agreement with Israel. And they lived very near Jerusalem. [2]So Adoni-Zedek and his people were very afraid because of this. Gibeon was not a little town like Ai. It was a large city. It was as big as a city that had a king. All its men were good fighters. ³So Adoni-Zedek king of Jerusalem sent a message to Hoham king of Hebron. He also sent it to Piram king of Jarmuth, Japhia king of Lachish, and Debir king of Eglon. The king of Jerusalem begged these men, ⁴"Come with me and help me attack Gibeon. Gibeon has made a peace agreement with Joshua and the Israelites."

Then these five Amorite kings joined their armies. They were the kings of Jerusalem, Hebron, Jarmuth, Lachish and Eglon. These armies went to Gibeon, surrounded it and attacked it.

⁶The Gibeonites sent a message to Joshua in his camp at Gilgal. The message said: "We are your servants. Don't let us be destroyed. Come quickly and help us! Save us! All the Amorite kings from the mountains have joined their armies. They are fighting against us."

⁷So Joshua marched out of Gilgal with his whole army. His best fighting men were with him. ⁸The Lord said to Joshua, "Don't be afraid of those armies. I will allow you to defeat them. None of them will be able to defeat you."

⁹Joshua and his army marched all night to Gibeon. So Joshua surprised them when he attacked. ¹⁰The Lord confused those armies when Israel attacked. So Israel defeated them in a great victory. They chased them from Gibeon on the road going to Beth Horon. . . . ¹¹They chased the enemy down the road from Beth Horon to Azekah. While they were chasing them, the Lord threw large hailstones on them from the sky. Many of the enemy

were killed by the hailstones. More men were killed by the hailstones than the Israelites killed with their swords.

¹²That day the Lord allowed the Israelites to defeat the Amorites. And that day Joshua stood before all the people of Israel and said to the Lord:

"Sun, stand still over Gibeon.

Moon, stand still over the Valley of Aijalon."

¹³So the sun stood still.

And the moon stopped

until the people defeated their

enemies.

These words are written in the Book of Jashar.

The sun stopped in the middle of the sky. It waited to go down for a full day. ¹⁴That has never happened at any time before that day or since. That was the day the Lord listened to a man. Truly the Lord was fighting for Israel!

We Will Serve the Lord!

(From Joshua 24)

24:¹ᵃ Then all the tribes of Israel met together at Shechem.

²Then Joshua spoke to all the people. He said, "Here's what the Lord, the God of Israel, says to you:

'A long time ago your ancestors lived on the other side of the Euphrates River. . . . They worshiped other gods. ³But I, the Lord, took your ancestor Abraham out of the land on the other side of the river. I led him through the land of Canaan. And I gave him many children. I gave him his son Isaac. ⁴And I gave Isaac two sons named Jacob and Esau. I gave the land around the mountains of Edom to Esau. But Jacob and his sons went down to Egypt. ⁵Then I sent Moses and Aaron to Egypt. I caused many terrible things to happen to the Egyptians. Then I brought you people out. ⁶When I brought your fathers out of Egypt, they came to the Red Sea. And the Egyptians chased them. There were chariots and men on horses. ⁷So the people asked me, the Lord, for help. And I caused great trouble to come to the Egyptians. I caused the sea to cover them. You yourselves saw what I did to the army of Egypt. After that, you lived in the desert for a long time.

⁸" 'Then I brought you to the land of the Amorites. This was east of the Jordan River. They fought against you, but I gave you the power to defeat them. I destroyed them before you. Then you took control of that land. ⁹But the king of Moab, Balak son of Zippor, prepared to fight against the Israelites. The king sent for Balaam son of Beor to

curse you. ¹⁰But I, the Lord, refused to listen to Balaam. So he asked for good things to happen to you! He blessed you many times. I saved you and brought you out of his power.

¹¹" 'Then you traveled across the Jordan River and came to Jericho. The people in the city of Jericho fought against you. . . . But I allowed you to defeat them all. ¹³ᵃIt was I, the Lord, who gave you that land. I gave you land where you did not have to work. I gave you cities that you did not have to build. And now you live in that land and in those cities.' "

¹⁴Then Joshua spoke to the people. He said, "Now you have heard the Lord's words. So you must respect the Lord and serve him fully and sincerely. Throw away the false gods that your people worshiped. . . . Now you must serve the Lord. ¹⁵But maybe you don't want to serve the Lord. You must choose for yourselves today. You must decide whom you will serve. You may serve the gods that your people worshiped when they lived on the other side of the Euphrates River. Or you may serve the gods of the Amorites who lived in this land. As for me and my family, we will serve the Lord."

Deborah and Barak
(From Judges 2 and 4)

2:⁷ᵃThe people of Israel served the Lord as long as Joshua was alive. They continued serving the Lord during the lifetimes of the older leaders who lived on after Joshua. [8]Joshua son of Nun was the servant of the Lord. Joshua died at the age of 110. [9]So the Israelites buried him in the land he had been given. That land was at Timnath Heres. It was in the mountains of Ephraim, north of Mount Gaash.

[10]After those people had died, their children grew up. They did not know the Lord or what he had done for Israel. [12b]They began to worship the gods of the people who lived around them. That made the Lord angry. [15b]So the Israelites suffered very much. [16a]Then the Lord chose leaders called judges. [17a]But the Israelites did not listen to their judges. They were not faithful to God. [18]Many times the enemies of Israel hurt the Israelites. So the Israelites would cry for help. And each time the Lord felt sorry for them. Each time he sent a judge to save them from their enemies. The Lord was with those judges. [19a]But when each judge died, the Israelites again sinned and worshiped the false gods.

4:[4]There was a prophetess named Deborah. She was the wife of Lappidoth. She was [a] judge of Israel at that time. [5]Deborah would sit under the Palm Tree of Deborah. . . . And the people of Israel would come to her to settle their arguments.

[6]Deborah sent a message to a man named Barak. . . . Deborah said to Barak, "The Lord, the God of Israel, commands you: 'Go and gather 10,000 men of Naphtali and Zebulun. Lead them to Mount Tabor. [7]I will make Sisera, the commander of Jabin's army, come to you. Sisera, his chariots and

his army will meet you at the Kishon River. I will help you to defeat Sisera there.'"

⁸Then Barak said to Deborah, "I will go if you will go with me. But if you will not go with me, I won't go."

⁹"Of course I will go with you," Deborah answered. . . . So Deborah went with Barak to Kedesh. ¹⁰At Kedesh, Barak called the people of Zebulun and Naphtali together. From them, he gathered 10,000 men to follow him. Deborah went with Barak also.

¹²Then Sisera was told that Barak son of Abinoam had gone up to Mount Tabor. ¹³ᵃSo Sisera gathered his 900 iron chariots and all the men with him.

¹⁴Then Deborah said to Barak, "Get up! Today is the day the Lord will help you defeat Sisera. You know the Lord has already cleared the way for you." So Barak led 10,000 men down from Mount Tabor. ¹⁵ᵃHe and his men attacked Sisera and his men. During the battle the Lord confused Sisera and his army and chariots. So Barak and his men used their swords to defeat Sisera's army.

God Calls Gideon

(From Judges 6)

6:¹¹The angel of the Lord came and sat down under an oak tree at Ophrah. . . . Gideon was separating some wheat from the chaff in a winepress. Gideon did this to keep wheat from the Midianites. ¹²The angel of the Lord appeared to Gideon and said, "The Lord is with you, mighty warrior!"

¹³Then Gideon said, "Pardon me, sir. If the Lord is with us, why are we having so many troubles? Our ancestors told us he did miracles. They told us the Lord brought them out of Egypt. But now he has left us. He has allowed the Midianites to defeat us."

¹⁴The Lord turned to Gideon and said, "You have the strength to save the people of Israel. Go and save them from the Midianites. I am the one who is sending you."

¹⁵But Gideon answered, "Pardon me, Lord. How can I save Israel? My family group is the weakest in Manasseh. And I am the least important member of my family."

¹⁶The Lord answered him, "I will be with you. It will seem as if you are fighting only one man."

¹⁷Then Gideon said to the Lord, "If you are pleased with me, give me proof. Show me that it is really you talking with me. ¹⁸Please wait here. Do not go away until I come back to you. Let me bring my offering and set it in front of you."

And the Lord said, "I will wait until you come back."

¹⁹So Gideon went in and cooked a young goat. He

also took about 20 quarts of flour and made bread without yeast. Then he put the meat into a basket. And he put the broth from the boiled meat into a pot. He brought out the meat, the broth and the bread without yeast. He brought the food to the angel of the Lord. Gideon gave it to him under the oak tree.

[20]The angel of God said to Gideon, "Put the meat and the bread without yeast on that rock over there. Then pour the broth on them." And Gideon did as he was told. [21]The angel of the Lord had a stick in his hand. He touched the meat and the bread with the end of the stick. Then fire jumped up from the rock! The meat and the bread were completely burned up! And the angel of the Lord disappeared! [22a]Then Gideon understood he had been talking to the angel of the Lord.

[24a]So Gideon built an altar there to worship the Lord. Gideon named the altar The Lord Is Peace.

[33]All the Midianites, the Amalekites, and other peoples from the east joined together. They came across the Jordan River and camped in the Valley of Jezreel. [34]But the Spirit of the Lord 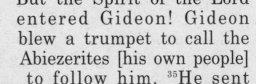 entered Gideon! Gideon blew a trumpet to call the Abiezerites [his own people] to follow him. [35]He sent messengers to all of Manasseh. The people of Manasseh were called to follow Gideon. Gideon also sent messen-

gers to the people of Asher, Zebulun and Naphtali. They also went up to meet Gideon and his men.

Gideon Puts a Fleece
Before the Lord
(From Judges 6 and 7)

6:³⁶Then Gideon said to God, "You said you would help me save Israel. ³⁷I will put some wool on the threshing floor. Let there be dew only on the wool. But let all of the ground be dry. Then I will know what you said is true. I will know that you will use me to save Israel." ³⁸And that is just what happened. Gideon got up early the next morning and squeezed the wool. He got a full bowl of water from the wool.

³⁹Then Gideon said to God, "Don't be angry with me. Let me ask just one more thing. Please let me make one more test. Let the wool be dry while the ground around it gets wet with dew." ⁴⁰That night God did that very thing. Just the wool was dry, but the ground around it was wet with dew.

7:[1a]Early in the morning [Gideon] and all his men set up their camp at the spring of Harod. [2]Then the Lord said to Gideon, "You have too many men to defeat the Midianites. I don't want the Israelites to brag that they saved themselves. [3]So now, announce to the people, 'Anyone who is afraid may leave Mount Gilead. He may go back home.'" And 22,000 men went back home. But 10,000 remained.

[4a]Then the Lord said to Gideon, "There are still too many men. Take the men down to the water, and I will test them for you there."

[5]So Gideon led the men down to the water. There the Lord said to him, "Separate them. Those who drink water by lapping it up like a dog will be in one group. Those who bend down to drink will be in the other group."

[7]Then the Lord said to Gideon, "I will save you, using the 300 men who lapped the water. And I will allow you to defeat Midian. Let all the other men go to their homes."

[9a]That night the Lord spoke to Gideon. He said, "Get up. Go down and attack the camp of the Midianites. [10]But if you are afraid to go down, take your servant Purah with you. [11a]When you come to the camp of Midian, you will hear what they are saying."

[13a]When Gideon came to the enemy camp, he heard a man talking. That man was telling his friend about a dream.

[14]The man's friend said, "Your dream is about the sword of Gideon son of Joash, a man of Israel. God will let Gideon defeat Midian and the whole army!"

[15b]Then Gideon went back to the camp of Israel.

He called out to them, "Get up! The Lord has defeated the army of Midian for you!" [16]Then Gideon divided the 300 men into three groups. He gave each man a trumpet and an empty jar. A burning torch was inside each jar.

[17]Gideon told the men, " . . . [18]Surround the enemy camp. I and everyone with me will blow our trumpets. When we blow our trumpets, you blow your trumpets, too. Then shout, 'For the Lord and for Gideon!'"

[19b]Then Gideon and his men blew their trumpets and smashed their jars. [22] . . . The Lord caused all the men of Midian to fight each other with their swords! The enemy army ran away. . . .

Samson and Delilah

(From Judges 16)

16:[4a]After this, Samson [a judge of Israel] fell in love with a woman named Delilah. [5]The kings of the Philistines went to Delilah. They said, "Try to find out what makes Samson so strong. . . . If you do this, each one of us will give you 28 pounds of silver."

[6]So Delilah said to Samson, "Tell me why you are so strong. How could someone tie you up and take control of you?"

[7]Samson answered, "Someone would have to . . . use seven new bowstrings that have not been dried. If he did that, I would be as weak as any other man."

⁸Then the kings of the Philistines brought seven new bowstrings to Delilah. They had not been dried. She tied Samson with them. ⁹ᵃSome men were hiding in another room. Delilah said to Samson, "Samson, the Philistines are about to capture you!" But Samson easily broke the bowstrings.

¹⁵Then Delilah said to him, "How can you say, 'I love you,' when you don't even trust me? . . . You haven't told me the secret of your great strength." ¹⁶ᵃShe kept bothering Samson about his secret day after day.

¹⁷ᵃSo he told her everything. He said, "I have never had my hair cut. I have been set apart to God as a Nazirite since I was born. If someone shaved my head, then I would lose my strength."

¹⁸ᵃDelilah . . . sent a message to the kings of the  Philistines. She said, "Come back one more time. He has told me everything." ¹⁹Delilah got Samson to go to sleep. . . . Then she called in a man to shave off . . . Samson's hair. . . . And Samson's strength left him.

²¹Then the Philistines captured Samson. They tore out his eyes. And they took him down to Gaza. They put bronze chains on him. They put him in prison and made him grind grain. ²²But his hair began to grow again.

²³The kings of the Philistines gathered to cele-

brate. They were going to offer a great sacrifice to their god Dagon. They said, "Our god has given us Samson our enemy."

[25a]The people were having a good time at the celebration. They said, "Bring Samson out to perform for us." So they brought Samson from the prison. [26]A servant was holding his hand. Samson said to him, "Let me feel the pillars that hold up the temple. I want to lean against them." [27a]Now the temple was full of men and women. All the kings of the Philistines were there. [28]Then Samson prayed to the Lord. He said, "Lord God, remember me. God, please give me strength one more time. Let me pay these Philistines back for putting out my two eyes!" [29]Then Samson held the two center pillars of the temple. These two pillars supported the whole temple. . . . His right hand was on one, and his left hand was on the other. [30]Samson said, "Let me die with these Philistines!" Then he pushed as hard as he could. And the temple fell on the kings and all the people in it. So Samson killed more of the Philistines when he died than when he was alive.

Ruth and Naomi
(From Ruth 1)

1:[1-2a]Long ago the judges ruled Israel. During their rule, there was a time in the land when there was not enough food to eat. A man named Elimelech left Bethlehem in Judah and moved to the country of Moab. He took his wife and his two sons with him. His wife was named Naomi, and his two sons were named Mahlon and Kilion.

³Later, Naomi's husband, Elimelech, died. So only Naomi and her two sons were left. ⁴These sons married women from Moab. The name of one wife was Orpah. The name of the other wife was Ruth. Naomi and her sons lived in Moab about ten years. ⁵Then Mahlon and Kilion also died. So Naomi was left alone without her husband or her two sons.

⁶While Naomi was in Moab, she heard that the Lord had taken care of his people. He had given food to them in Judah. So Naomi got ready to leave Moab and go back home. The wives of Naomi's sons also got ready to go with her. ⁷So they left the place where they had lived. And they started back on the way to the land of Judah. ⁸But Naomi said to her two daughters-in-law, "Go back home. Each of you go to your own mother's house. You have been very kind to me and to my sons who are now dead. I hope the Lord will also be kind to you in the same way. ⁹I hope the Lord will give you another home and a new husband."

Then Naomi kissed the women. And they began to cry out loud. ¹⁰Her daughters-in-law said to her, "No. We will go with you to your people."

¹¹ᵃBut Naomi said, "My daughters, go back to your own homes. Why do you want to go with me? ¹³ᵇMy life is much too sad for you to share. This is because the Lord is against me!"

¹⁴The women cried together again. Then Orpah kissed Naomi good-bye, but Ruth held on to her.

¹⁵Naomi said, "Look, your sister-in-law is going back

to her own people and her own gods. Go back with her."

[16]But Ruth said, "Don't ask me to leave you! Don't beg me not to follow you! Every place you go, I will go. Every place you live, I will live. Your people will be my people. Your God will be my God. [17]And where you die, I will die. And there I will be buried. I ask the Lord to punish me terribly if I do not keep this promise: Only death will separate us."

[18]Naomi saw that Ruth had made up her mind to go with her. So Naomi stopped arguing with her. [19a]Naomi and Ruth went on until they came to the town of Bethlehem.

[22]So Naomi and her daughter-in-law Ruth, the woman from Moab, came back from Moab. They came to Bethlehem at the beginning of the barley harvest.

Ruth and Boaz

(From Ruth 2 and 4)

2:[1]Now there was a rich man living in Bethlehem whose name was Boaz. Boaz was one of Naomi's close relatives from Elimelech's family.

[2]One day Ruth, the woman from Moab, said to Naomi, "Let me go to the fields. Maybe someone

will be kind and let me gather the grain he leaves in his field."

Naomi said, "Go, my daughter."

³So Ruth went to the fields. She followed the workers who were cutting the grain. And she gathered the grain that they had left. It just so happened that the field belonged to Boaz. He was a close relative from Elimelech's family.

⁴When Boaz came from Bethlehem, he spoke to his workers: "The Lord be with you!"

And the workers answered, "May the Lord bless you!"

⁵Then Boaz spoke to his servant who was in charge of the workers. He asked, "Whose girl is that?"

⁶The servant answered, "She is the Moabite woman who came with Naomi from the country of Moab. ⁷She said, 'Please let me follow the workers and gather the grain that they leave on the ground.' She came and has remained here. From morning until just now, she has stopped only a few moments to rest in the shelter."

⁸ªThen Boaz said to Ruth, "Listen, my daughter. Stay here in my field to gather grain for yourself. Do not go to any other person's field."

¹⁰Then Ruth bowed low with her face to the ground. She said to Boaz, "I am a stranger. Why have you been so kind to notice me?"

¹¹Boaz answered her, "I know about all the help

you have given to Naomi, your mother-in-law. You helped her even after your husband died. You left your father and mother and your own country. You came to this nation where you did not know anyone. ¹²The Lord will reward you for all you have done. . . . You have come to him as a little bird finds shelter under the wings of its mother."

4:⁹ᵃ[A while later] Boaz spoke to the older leaders and to all the people. He said, " . . . ¹⁰ᵃI am . . . taking Ruth as my wife."

¹³So Boaz took Ruth and married her. The Lord let her become pregnant, and she gave birth to a son. ¹⁴The women told Naomi, "Praise the Lord who gave you this grandson. And may he become famous in Israel. ¹⁵He will give you new life. And he will take care of you in your old age. This happened because of your daughter-in-law. She loves you. And she is better for you than seven sons. She has given birth to your grandson."

¹⁶Naomi took the boy, held him in her arms and cared for him. ¹⁷The neighbors gave the boy his name. These women said, "This boy was born for Naomi." The neighbors named him Obed. Obed was Jesse's father. And Jesse was the father of David.

Hannah Prays for a Child

(From 1 Samuel 1)

1:⁹ᵇ Now Eli the priest was sitting on a chair near the entrance to the Lord's Holy Tent. ¹⁰Hannah [Elkanah's wife] was very sad. She cried much and prayed to the Lord. [11]She made a promise. She said, "Lord of heaven's armies, see how bad I feel. Remember me! Don't forget me. If you will give me a son, I will give him back to you all his life. And no one will ever use a razor to cut his hair."

[12]While Hanna kept praying, Eli watched her mouth. [13]She was praying in her heart. Her lips moved, but her voice was not heard. So Eli thought she was drunk. [14]He said to her, "Stop getting drunk! Throw away your wine!"

[15]Hannah answered, "No, master, I have not drunk any wine or beer. I am a woman who is deeply troubled. I was telling the Lord about all my problems. [16]Don't think of me as an evil woman. I have been praying because of my many troubles and much sadness."

[17]Eli answered, "Go in peace. May the God of Israel give you what you asked of him."

[18]Hannah said, "I want to be pleasing to you always." Then she left. . . . She was not sad anymore.

[19a]Early the next morning Elkanah's family got up and worshiped the Lord. Then they went back home to Ramah. [20]So Hannah became pregnant, and in time she gave birth to a son. She named him Samuel. She said, "His name is Samuel because I asked the Lord for him."

[21]Every year Elkanah went to Shiloh to offer sacrifices. He went to keep the promise he had made to God. He brought his whole family with him. So once again he went up to Shiloh. [22]But Hannah did not go with him. She told him, "When the boy is old enough to eat solid food, I will take him to Shiloh.

Then I will give him to the Lord. He will become a Nazirite. He will always live there at Shiloh."

²³Elkanah, Hannah's husband, said to her, "Do what you think is best. You may stay home until the boy is old enough to eat. May the Lord do what you have said." So Hannah stayed at home to nurse her son until he was old enough to eat.

²⁴When Samuel was old enough to eat, Hannah took him to the Tent of the Lord at Shiloh. She also took a three-year-old bull, one-half bushel of flour and a leather bag filled with wine. ²⁵They killed the bull for the sacrifice.

Then Hannah brought Samuel to Eli. ²⁶She said to Eli, "As surely as you live, my master, I am the same woman who stood near you praying to the Lord. ²⁷I prayed for this child. The Lord answered my prayer and gave him to me. ²⁸Now I give him back

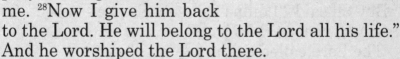

to the Lord. He will belong to the Lord all his life." And he worshiped the Lord there.

God Calls Samuel

(From 1 Samuel 2, 3, and 8)

2:¹² Now Eli's sons were evil men. They did not care about the Lord.

¹⁸But Samuel obeyed the Lord. He wore a linen holy vest. ¹⁹Every year Samuel's mother would make a little coat for him. She would take it to him when she went to Shiloh. She went there with her husband for the sacrifice. ²⁰Eli would bless Elkanah and his wife. Eli would say, "May the Lord repay you with children through Hannah. They will take the place of the boy Hannah prayed for and gave back to the Lord." Then Elkanah and Hannah would go home. ²¹The Lord was kind to Hannah. She became the mother of three sons and two daughters. And the boy Samuel grew up serving the Lord.

3:¹The boy Samuel served the Lord under Eli. In those days the Lord did not speak directly to people very often. There were very few visions.

²Eli's eyes were so weak he was almost blind. One night he was lying in bed. ³ᵃSamuel was also in bed in the Lord's Holy Tent.

⁴Then the Lord called Samuel. Samuel answered, "I am here!" ⁵He ran to Eli and said, "I am here. You called me."

But Eli said, "I didn't call you. Go back to bed." So Samuel went back to bed.

⁶The Lord called again, "Samuel!"

Samuel again went to Eli and said, "I am here. You called me."

Again Eli said, "I didn't call you. Go back to bed."

⁷Samuel did not yet know the Lord. The Lord had not spoken directly to him yet.

⁸The Lord called Samuel for the third time. Samuel got up and went to Eli. He said, "I am here. You called me."

Then Eli realized the Lord was calling the boy. [9]So he told Samuel, "Go to bed. If he calls you again, say, 'Speak, Lord. I am your servant, and I am listening.'" So Samuel went and lay down in bed.

[10]The Lord came and stood there. He called as he had before. He said, "Samuel, Samuel!"

Samuel said, "Speak, Lord. I am your servant, and I am listening."

[19]The Lord was with Samuel as he grew up. He did not let any of Samuel's messages fail to come true. [20]Then all Israel, from Dan to Beersheba, knew Samuel was a prophet of the Lord. [21]And the Lord continued to show himself to Samuel at Shiloh. He also showed himself to Samuel through his word.

8:[1]When Samuel became old, he made his sons judges for Israel. [3]But Samuel's sons did not live as he did. They tried to get money dishonestly. They took money secretly to be dishonest in their judging.

[4]So all the older leaders came together and met Samuel at Ramah. [5]They said to him, "You're old, and your sons don't live as you do. Give us a king to rule over us like all the other nations."

[21]Samuel heard all that the people said. Then he repeated all their words to the Lord. [22]The Lord answered, "You must listen to them. Give them a king."

Samuel Appoints a King

(From 1 Samuel 10, 13, 15, and 16)

10:¹Samuel took a jar of olive oil. He poured the oil on Saul's head. He kissed Saul and said, "The Lord has appointed you to be leader of his people Israel. You will rule over the people of the Lord. You will save them from their enemies all around."

13:¹Saul was 30 years old when he became king. He was king over Israel 42 years.

15:¹⁰Then the Lord spoke his word to Samuel: ¹¹"Saul has stopped following me. And I am sorry I made him king. He has not obeyed my commands." Samuel was upset, and he cried out to the Lord all night long.

16:¹The Lord said to Samuel, "How long will you continue to feel sorry for Saul? I have rejected him as king of Israel. Fill your container with olive oil and go. I am sending you to Jesse who lives in Bethlehem. I have chosen one of his sons to be king."

⁴Samuel did what the Lord told him to do. When he arrived at Bethlehem, the older leaders of Bethlehem shook with fear. They met him and asked, "Are you coming in peace?"

⁵Samuel answered, "Yes, I come in peace. I have come to make a sacrifice to the Lord. Make yourselves holy for the Lord and come to the sacrifice with me." Then he made Jesse and his sons holy for the Lord. And he invited them to come to the sacrifice.

⁶When they arrived, Samuel saw Eliab. Samuel

thought, "Surely the Lord has appointed this person standing here before him."

⁷But the Lord said to Samuel, "Don't look at how handsome Eliab is. Don't look at how tall he is. I have not chosen him. God does not see the same way people see. People look at the outside of a person, but the Lord looks at the heart."

⁸Then Jesse called Abinadab and told him to pass by Samuel. But Samuel said, "The Lord has not chosen this man either." ⁹Then Jesse had Shammah pass by. But Samuel said, "No, the Lord has not chosen this one." ¹⁰Jesse had seven of his sons pass by Samuel. But Samuel said to him, "The Lord has not chosen any of these."

¹¹Then he asked Jesse, "Are these all the sons you have?"

Jesse answered, "I still have the youngest son. He is out taking care of the sheep."

Samuel said, "Send for him. We will not sit down to eat until he arrives."

¹²So Jesse sent and had his youngest son brought in. He was a fine boy, tanned and handsome.

The Lord said to Samuel, "Go! Appoint him. He is the one."

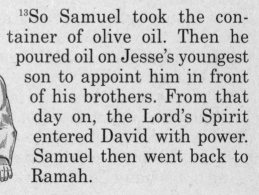

¹³So Samuel took the container of olive oil. Then he poured oil on Jesse's youngest son to appoint him in front of his brothers. From that day on, the Lord's Spirit entered David with power. Samuel then went back to Ramah.

David and Goliath

(From 1 Samuel 17)

17:⁴The Philistines had a champion fighter named Goliath. He was from Gath. He was about nine feet four inches tall. He came out of the Philistine camp.

⁸Goliath stood and shouted to the Israelite soldiers, "Why have you taken positions for battle? I am a Philistine, and you are Saul's servants! Choose a man and send him to fight me."

²⁶David asked the men who stood near him, "What will be done to reward the man who kills this Philistine? . . . Why does [Goliath] think he can speak against the armies of the living God?"

³¹Some men heard what David said and told Saul. Then Saul ordered David to be sent to him.

³²David said to Saul, "Don't let anyone be discouraged. I, your servant, will go and fight this Philistine!

³⁷"The Lord saved me from a lion and a bear. He will also save me from this Philistine."

Saul said to David, "Go, and may the Lord be with you." ³⁸Saul put his own clothes on David. He put a bronze helmet on David's head and armor on his body. ³⁹David put on Saul's sword and tried to walk around. But he was not used to all the armor Saul had put on him.

He said to Saul, "I can't go in this. I'm not used to it." Then David took it all off. ⁴⁰He took his stick in his hand. And he chose five smooth stones from a stream. He put them in his pouch and held his sling in his hand. Then he went to meet Goliath.

⁴¹At the same time, the Philistine was coming closer to David. The man who held his shield walked in front of him. ⁴²Goliath looked at David. He saw that David was only a boy, tanned and handsome. He looked down at David with disgust. ⁴³He said, "Do you think I am a dog, that you come at me with a stick?" He used his gods' names to curse David. ⁴⁴He said to David, "Come here. I'll feed your body to the birds of the air and the wild animals!"

⁴⁵But David said to him, "You come to me using a sword, a large spear and a small spear. But I come to you in the name of the Lord of heaven's armies. He's the God of the armies of Israel! You have spoken out against him. ⁴⁶Today the Lord will give you to me. . . . Then all the world will know there is a God in Israel! ⁴⁷Everyone gathered here will know the Lord does not need swords or spears to save people. The battle belongs to him! And he will help us defeat all of you."

⁴⁸As Goliath came near to attack him, David ran quickly to meet him. ⁴⁹He took a stone from his pouch. He put it into his sling and slung it. The stone hit the Philistine on his forehead and sank into it. Goliath fell facedown on the ground.

⁵⁰So David defeated the Philistine with only a sling and a stone! He hit him and killed him. He did not even have a sword in his hand.

Saul Grows Angry

(From 1 Samuel 18, 19, and 24)

18:⁵Saul sent David to fight in different battles. And David was very successful. Then Saul put David over the soldiers. When he did this, Saul's officers and all the other people were pleased.

⁶After David had killed the Philistine, he and the men returned home. Women came out from all the towns of Israel to meet King Saul. They sang songs of joy, danced and played tambourines and stringed instruments. ⁷As they played, they sang,

"Saul has killed thousands of his enemies,
But David has killed tens of thousands!"

⁸The women's song upset Saul, and he became very angry. He thought, "The women say David has killed tens of thousands of enemies. But they say I killed only thousands of enemies. The only thing left for him to have is the kingdom!" ⁹So Saul watched David closely from then on. He was jealous of him.

³⁰The Philistine commanders continued to go out to fight the Israelites. But every time, David defeated them. He had more success than Saul's officers. And he became famous.

19:¹Saul told his son Jonathan and all his servants to kill David. But Jonathan cared very much for David. ²ᵃSo he warned David.

¹⁸ᵃAfter David had escaped from Saul, he went to Samuel at Ramah. He told Samuel everything Saul had done to him.

24:¹Now Saul . . . was told, "David is in the desert of En Gedi." ²So he chose 3,000 men from all Israel. He took these men and began looking for David and his men. They looked near the Rocks of the Wild Goats.

³Saul came to the sheep pens beside the road. A cave was there, and he went in to relieve himself. Now David and his men were hiding far back in the cave. ⁴The men said to David, "Today is the day the Lord talked about! The Lord told you, 'I will give your enemy to you. You can do anything you want with him.'"

Then David crawled near Saul. He cut off a corner of Saul's robe. But Saul did not notice him. ⁷ᵇThen Saul left the cave and went his way.

⁸When David came out of the cave, he shouted to Saul, "My master and king!" Saul looked back, and David bowed facedown on the ground. ⁹He said to Saul, "Why do you listen when people say, 'David plans to harm you'? ¹⁰ᵇYou have seen how the Lord put you in my power in the cave. But I refused to kill you. I was merciful to you. . . . ¹¹ᵇI cut off the corner of your robe, but I didn't kill you."

¹⁶David finished saying these words. Then Saul asked, "Is that your voice, David my son?" And he cried loudly. ¹⁷He said, "You are right, and I am wrong. You have been good to me. But I have done

wrong to you. [19b]May the Lord reward you because you were good to me today."

[22b]Then Saul went back home. David and his men went up to the protected place.

David Becomes King

(From 1 Samuel 31 and 2 Samuel 1 and 2)

31:[1]The Philistines fought against Israel, and the Israelites ran away from them. Many Israelites were killed at Mount Gilboa. [2]The Philistines fought hard against Saul and his sons. They killed his sons Jonathan, Abinadab and Malki-Shua. [3]The fighting became bad around Saul. When the archers shot at him, he was badly wounded. [4]He said to the officer who carried his armor, "Pull out your sword and kill me. Then those . . . men won't make fun of me and kill me." But Saul's officer refused, because he was afraid. So Saul took his own sword and threw himself on it. [5]The officer saw that Saul was dead. So he threw himself on his own sword. And he died with Saul. [6]So Saul, his three sons and the officer who carried his armor died together that day.

[7]Now there were Israelites who lived on the other side of Jezreel Valley. And some lived across the Jordan River. They saw how the Israelite army had run away. And they saw that Saul and his sons were dead. So they left their cities and ran away. Then the Philistines came and lived there.

1:¹Now Saul was dead. And after David had defeated the Amalekites, he returned to Ziklag. He stayed there two days. ²On the third day a young man came to Ziklag. He came from Saul's camp. To show his sadness his clothes were torn, and he had dirt on his head. He came and bowed facedown on the ground before David.

³David asked him, "Where did you come from?"

The man answered, "I escaped from the Israelite camp."

⁴David asked him, "What happened? Please tell me!"

The man answered, "The people have run away from the battle. Many of them have fallen dead. Saul and his son Jonathan are dead also."

¹¹Then David tore his clothes to show his sorrow. And all the men with him did also. ¹²They were very sad and cried. They did not eat until evening. They cried for Saul and his son Jonathan. And they cried for the Israelites who had been killed with swords.

2:¹Later, David prayed to the Lord. David said, "Should I go up to any of the cities of Judah?"

The Lord said to David, "Go."

David asked, "Where should I go?"

The Lord answered, "To Hebron."

²ªSo David went up to Hebron with his two wives. ³David also brought his men and their families. They all made their homes in the cities of Hebron. ⁴Then the men of Judah came to Hebron. They appointed David king over Judah.

They told David that the men of Jabesh Gilead had buried Saul. ⁵So David sent messengers to the men of Jabesh Gilead. They told David's message to the men in Jabesh: "The Lord bless you. You have shown kindness to your master Saul by burying him. ⁶May the Lord now be kind and true to you. I will also be kind to you because you have done this. ⁷Now be strong and brave. Saul your master is dead. The people of Judah have appointed me their king."

David Wants to Build a Temple for God

(From 2 Samuel 7)

7:¹King David was living in his palace. And the Lord gave him peace from all his enemies around him. ²David said to Nathan the prophet, "Look, I am living in a palace made of cedar wood. But the Holy Box of God is still kept in a tent!"

³Nathan said to the king, "Go and do what you really want to do. The Lord is with you."

⁴But that night the Lord spoke his word to Nathan. The Lord said, ⁵"Go and tell my servant David, 'This is what the Lord says: You are not the person to build a house for me to live in. ⁶I did not live in a house when I brought the Israelites out of Egypt. I have been moving around all this time with a tent as my home. ⁷I have continued to move

with the tribes of Israel. But I have never asked their leaders who take care of them to build me a house of cedar wood.'

⁸"You must tell my servant David, 'This is what the Lord of heaven's armies says: I took you from the pasture when you were following the sheep. I took you to become leader of my people, the Israelites. ⁹I have been with you everywhere you have gone. I have defeated your enemies for you. I will make you as famous as any of the great men on the earth. ¹⁰Also I will choose a place for my people, the Israelites. I will plant them so they can live in their own home. They will not be bothered anymore. Wicked people will no longer make them suffer as they have in the past. ¹¹Wicked people continued to do this even when I appointed judges. But I will give you peace from all your enemies. I also tell you that I will make your descendants kings of Israel after you.

¹²"'Your days will come to an end, and you will die. At that time I will make one of your sons the next king. ¹³He will build a temple for me. I will make his kingdom strong forever. ¹⁴ᵃI will be his father, and he will be my son. ¹⁶ . . . Your family and your kingdom will continue forever before me. Your rule will last forever.'"

¹⁷Nathan told David everything he had heard.

^{18a}Then King David went in the tent and sat in front of the Lord. David said, ²¹"You have done this wonderful thing because you said you would. You have done it because you wanted to. And you have decided to let me know all these great things. ²²This is why you are great, Lord God! There is no one like you. There is no God except you. We have heard all this ourselves! ²³And there are no others like your people, the Israelites. They are the one nation on earth that God chose to be his people. You used them to make your name well-known. You did great and wonderful miracles for them. . . . You freed your people from slavery in Egypt. ²⁴You made the people of Israel your very own people forever. And, Lord, you became their God."

David and Mephibosheth

(From 2 Samuel 9)

9:¹David asked, "Is there anyone still left in Saul's family? I want to show kindness to this person for Jonathan's sake!"

²Now there was a servant named Ziba from Saul's family. So David's servants called Ziba to him. King David said to him, "Are you Ziba?"

He answered, "Yes, I am Ziba, your servant."

³The king asked, "Is there anyone left in Saul's family? I want to show God's kindness to this person."

Ziba answered the king, "Jonathan has a son still living. He is crippled in both feet."

⁴The king asked Ziba, "Where is this son?"

Ziba answered, "He is at the house of Makir son of Ammiel in Lo Debar."

⁵Then King David had servants bring Jonathan's son from the house of Makir son of Ammiel in Lo Debar. ⁶Mephibosheth, Jonathan's son, came before David and bowed facedown on the floor.

David said, "Mephibosheth!"

Mephibosheth said, "I am your servant."

⁷David said to him, "Don't be afraid. I will be kind to you for your father Jonathan's sake. I will give you back all the land of your grandfather Saul. And you will always be able to eat at my table."

⁸Mephibosheth bowed to David again. Mephibosheth said, "You are being very kind to me, your servant! And I am no better than a dead dog!"

⁹Then King David called Saul's servant Ziba. David said to him, "I have given your master's grandson everything that belonged to Saul and his family. ¹⁰You, your sons and your servants will farm the land for Mephibosheth. You will harvest the crops. Then your master's grandson will

have food to eat. But Mephibosheth, your master's grandson, will always be able to eat at my table."

(Now Ziba had 15 sons and 20 servants.) ¹¹Ziba said to King David, "I am your servant. I will do everything my master, the king, commands me."

So Mephibosheth ate at David's table as if he were one of the king's sons. ¹²Mephibosheth had a young son named Mica. Everyone in Ziba's family became Mephibosheth's servants. ¹³Mephibosheth was crippled in both feet. He lived in Jerusalem and always ate at the king's table.

Solomon Becomes King

(From 1 Kings 2 and 3)

2:¹ It was almost time for David to die. So he talked to Solomon [his son] and gave him his last commands. ²David said, "My time to die is near. Be a good and strong leader. ³ᵃObey everything that the Lord commands. . . . Obey all his laws, and do what he told us."

¹⁰Then David died and was buried with his ancestors in Jerusalem. ¹¹ᵃHe had ruled over Israel 40 years.

¹²Now Solomon became king after David, his father. And he was in firm control of his kingdom.

3:⁴ᵃ King Solomon went to Gibeon to offer a sacrifice. ⁵While he was at Gibeon, the Lord came to him in a dream during the night. God said, "Ask for anything you want. I will give it to you."

⁶Solomon answered, "You were very kind to your servant, my father David. He obeyed you. . . . And

you showed great kindness to him when you allowed his son to be king after him. [7b]But . . . I do not have the wisdom I need to do what I must do. [9a]So I ask that you give me wisdom. Then I can rule the people in the right way."

[10]The Lord was pleased that Solomon had asked him for this. [11a]So God said to him, [12]"I will give you what you asked. . . . Your wisdom will be greater than anyone has had in the past. And there will never be anyone in the future like you."

[16]One day two women . . . came to Solomon. They stood before him. [17]One of the women said, "My master, this woman and I live in the same house. I gave birth to a baby while she was there with me. [18]Three days later this woman also gave birth to a baby. No one else was in the house with us. There were only the two of us. [19]One night this woman rolled over on her baby, and it died. [20]So during the night she took my son from my bed while I was asleep. She carried him to her bed. Then she put the dead baby in my bed. [21]The next morning I got up to feed my baby. But I saw that he was dead! Then I looked at him more closely. I saw that he was not my son."

[22]But the other woman said, "No! The living baby is my son. The dead baby is yours!"

But the first woman said, "No! The dead baby is

yours, and the living one is mine!" So the two women argued before the king.

²⁴Then King Solomon sent his servants to get a sword. When they brought it to him, ²⁵he said, "Cut the living baby into two pieces. Give each woman half of the baby."

²⁶The real mother of the living child was full of love for her son. She said to the king, "Please, my master, don't kill him! Give the baby to her!"

But the other woman said, "Neither of us will have him. Cut him into two pieces!"

²⁷Then King Solomon said, "Give the baby to the first woman. Don't kill him. She is the real mother."

²⁸When the people of Israel heard about King Solomon's decision, they respected him very much. They saw he had wisdom from God to make the right decisions.

Solomon Builds the Temple
(From 1 Kings 6)

6:¹ᵃSo Solomon began to build the Temple. This was 480 years after the people of Israel had left Egypt. (This was the fourth year of King Solomon's rule over Israel.)

²The Temple was 90 feet long and 30 feet wide. It was 45 feet high. ³The porch in front of the main room of the Temple was 15 feet deep and 30 feet wide The room ran along the front of the Temple itself. Its width was equal to the width of the Temple. ⁴There were narrow windows in the

Temple. These windows were narrow on the outside and larger on the inside.

¹¹The Lord spoke his word to Solomon: ¹²"Obey all my laws and commands. If you do, I will do for you what I promised your father David. ¹³And I will live among the children of Israel in this Temple you are building. I will never leave the people of Israel."

¹⁴So Solomon finished building the Temple.

¹⁹He prepared the inner room at the back of the Temple to keep the Box of the Agreement with the Lord. ²⁰This inner room was 30 feet long, 30 feet wide and 30 feet high. Solomon covered this room with pure gold. He built an altar of cedar and covered it also. ²¹He covered the inside of the Temple with pure gold. And he placed gold chains across the front of the inner room. It was also covered with gold. ²²So all the inside of the Temple was covered with gold. Also the altar in the Most Holy Place was covered with gold.

²³Solomon made two creatures with wings from olive wood. Each creature was 15 feet tall. They were put in the Most Holy Place. ²⁴Each creature had two wings. Each wing was 7½ feet long. So it was 15 feet from the end of one wing to the end of the other wing. ²⁵The creatures were the same size and shape. ²⁶And each was 15 feet tall. ²⁷These

creatures were put beside each other in the Most Holy Place. Their wings were spread out. So one creature's wing touched one wall. The other creature's wing touched the other wall. And their wings touched each other in the middle of the room. ²⁸The two creatures were covered with gold.

^{29a}All the walls around the Temple were carved. They were carved with pictures of creatures with wings, palm trees and flowers. ³⁰The floors of both rooms were covered with gold.

^{31a}Doors made from olive wood were put at the entrance to the Most Holy Place. ³²Creatures with wings, palm trees and flowers were carved on the two olive wood doors. Then the doors were covered with gold. And the creatures and the palm trees were covered with gold.

³⁷Work began on the Temple . . . during the fourth year Solomon ruled over Israel. ³⁸The Temple was finished during the eleventh year Solomon ruled. . . . It was finished exactly as it was planned. Solomon had worked seven years to build the Temple.

The Queen of Sheba Visits Solomon

(From 1 Kings 10)

10:¹Now the queen of Sheba heard about Solomon's fame. So she came to test him with hard questions. ²She traveled to Jerusalem with a very large group of servants. There were many camels carrying spices, jewels and much gold. She came to Solomon and talked with him about all that she had in mind. ³Solomon answered all her questions. Nothing was too hard for him to explain to her. ⁴The queen of Sheba learned that Solomon was very wise. She saw the palace he had built. ⁵She saw his many officers and the food on his table. She saw the palace servants and their good clothes. She was shown the servants who served him at feasts. And she was shown the  whole burnt offerings he made in the Temple of the Lord. All these things amazed her.

⁶So she said to King Solomon, "I heard in my own country about your achievements and wisdom. And all of it is true. ⁷I could not believe it then. But now I have come and seen it with my own eyes. I was not told even half of it! Your wisdom and wealth are much greater than I had heard. ⁸Your men and officers are very lucky! In always serving you, they are able to hear your wisdom! ⁹Praise the Lord your God! He was pleased to make you king of Israel. The Lord has constant love for Israel. So he made you king to keep justice and to rule fairly."

¹⁰Then the queen of Sheba gave the king about 9,000 pounds of gold. She also gave him many spices and jewels. No one since that time has brought more spices into Israel than the queen of Sheba gave King Solomon.

¹¹(Hiram's ships brought gold from Ophir. They also brought from there very much juniper wood and jewels. ¹²Solomon used the juniper wood to build supports for the Temple of the Lord and the palace. He also used it to make harps and lyres for the musicians. Such fine juniper wood has not been brought in or seen since that time.)

¹³King Solomon gave the queen of Sheba many gifts. He gave her gifts that a king would give to another ruler. Then he gave her whatever else she wanted and asked for. After this, she and her servants went back to her own country.

¹⁴Every year King Solomon received about 50,000 pounds of gold. ¹⁵Besides that he also received gold from the traders and merchants. And he received gold from the kings of Arabia and governors of the land.

²³So Solomon had more riches and wisdom than all the other kings on earth. ²⁴People everywhere wanted to see King Solomon. They wanted to hear the wisdom God had given him. ²⁵Every year everyone who came brought a gift. They brought things made of gold and silver, along with clothes, weapons, spices, horses and mules.

Elijah Fed by Ravens

(From 1 Kings 16 and 17)

16:²⁹ᵃAhab son of Omri became king of Israel. ³⁰Ahab did many things that the Lord said were wrong. He did more evil than any of the kings before him.

17:¹Now Elijah was a prophet from the town of Tishbe in Gilead. Elijah said to King Ahab, "I serve the Lord, the God of Israel. As surely as the Lord lives, I tell you the truth. No rain or dew will fall during the next few years unless I command it."

²Then the Lord spoke his word to Elijah: ³"Leave this place. Go east and hide near Kerith Ravine. It is east of the Jordan River. ⁴You may drink from the brook. And I have commanded ravens to bring you food there." ⁵So Elijah did what the Lord told him to do. He went to Kerith Ravine, east of the Jordan, and lived there. ⁶The birds brought Elijah bread and meat every morning and every evening. And he drank water from the brook.

⁷After a while the brook dried up because there was no rain. ⁸Then the Lord spoke his word to Elijah [the prophet], ⁹"Go to Zarephath in Sidon. Live there. I have commanded a widow there to take care of you."

¹⁰So Elijah went to Zarephath. When he reached the town gate, he saw a widow there. She was gathering wood for a fire. Elijah asked her, "Would you bring me a little water in a cup? I would like to have a drink." ¹¹As she was going to get his water, Elijah said, "Please bring me a piece of bread, too."

¹²The woman answered, "As surely as the Lord your God lives, I tell you the truth. I have no bread. I have only a handful of flour in a jar. And I have only a little olive oil in a jug. I came here to gather some wood. I will take it home and cook our last meal. My son and I will eat it and then die from hunger."

¹³Elijah said to her, "Don't worry. Go home and cook your food as you have said. But first make a small loaf of bread from the flour you have. Bring it to me. Then cook something for yourself and your son. ¹⁴The Lord, the God of Israel, says, 'That jar of flour will never become empty. The jug will always have oil in it. This will continue until the day the Lord sends rain to the land.'"

¹⁵So the woman went home. And she did what Elijah told her to do. So Elijah, the woman and her son had enough food every day. ¹⁶The jar of flour and the jug of oil were never empty. This happened just as the Lord, through Elijah, said it would.

¹⁷Some time later the son of the woman who owned the house became sick. He grew worse and worse. Finally he stopped breathing. ¹⁸So the woman said to Elijah, "You are a man of God. What have you done to me? Did you come here to remind me of my sin? Did you come here to kill my son?"

¹⁹Elijah said to her, "Give me your son." So Elijah took the boy from her and carried him upstairs. Elijah laid the boy on the bed in the room where he was staying. ²⁰Then he prayed to the Lord. He said, "Lord my God, this widow is letting me stay in her house. Why have you done this terrible thing to her? Why have you caused her son to die?" ²¹ᵇElijah prayed to the Lord, "Lord my God, let this boy live again!"

²²The Lord answered Elijah's prayer. The boy began breathing again, and he was alive. ²³Elijah carried the boy downstairs. He gave the boy to his mother and said, "See! Your son is alive!"

²⁴The woman said to Elijah, "Now I know you really are a man from God. I know that the Lord truly speaks through you!"

Elijah and the Prophets of Baal

(From 1 Kings 18)

18:¹During the third year without rain, the Lord spoke his word to Elijah: The Lord said, "Go and meet King Ahab. I will soon send rain." ²ᵃSo Elijah went to meet Ahab.

¹⁷When [Ahab] saw Elijah, he said, "Is it you—the biggest troublemaker in Israel?"

¹⁸Elijah answered, "I have not made trouble in Israel. You and your father's family have caused all this trouble. You have not obeyed the Lord's commands. You have followed the Baals. ¹⁹ᵃNow

tell all Israel to meet me at Mount Carmel. Also bring the 450 prophets of Baal there."

[20]So Ahab called all the Israelites and those prophets to Mount Carmel.

[22]Elijah said, "I am the only prophet of the Lord here. But there are 450 prophets of Baal. [23]So bring two bulls. Let the prophets of Baal choose one bull. . . . Then let them put the meat on the wood. But they are not to set fire to it. Then I will do the same with the other bull. And I will put the meat on the wood. But I will not set fire to it. [24a]You prophets of Baal, pray to your god. And I will pray to the Lord. The god who answers the prayer will set fire to his wood. He is the true God."

[26a]So [the prophets of Baal] took the bull that was given to them and prepared it. They prayed to Baal from morning until noon. They shouted, "Baal, answer us!" But there was no sound.

[27]At noon Elijah began to make fun of them. He said, "Pray louder! If Baal really is a god, maybe he is thinking. Or maybe he is busy or traveling! Maybe he is sleeping so you will have to wake him!" [28a]So the prophets prayed louder. [29]The afternoon passed, and the prophets continued to act wildly. . . . But no voice was heard. Baal did not answer. No one paid attention.

[30]Then Elijah said to all the people, "Now come to me." So they gathered around him. Elijah rebuilt the altar of the Lord because it had been torn down. [32b]Then he dug a small ditch around it. . . . [33]Elijah put the wood on the altar. He cut the bull into pieces and laid them on the wood. Then he

said, "Fill four jars with water. Put the water on the meat and on the wood."

³⁴Then Elijah said, "Do it again." And they did it again.

Then he said, "Do it a third time." And they did it the third time. ³⁵So the water ran off of the altar and filled the ditch.

³⁶ᵇSo the prophet Elijah went near the altar. He prayed, "Lord, you are the God of Abraham, Isaac and Israel. I ask you now to prove that you are the God of Israel. And prove that I am your servant. . . . ³⁷Lord, answer my prayer. . . . Then the people will know that you are bringing them back to you."

[38]Then fire from the Lord came down. It burned the sacrifice, the wood, the stones and the ground around the altar. It also dried up the water in the ditch. [39]When all the people saw this, they fell down to the ground. They cried, "The Lord is God! The Lord is God!"

Chariots of Fire

(From 2 Kings 2)

2:[1]It was near the time for the Lord to take Elijah. He was going to take him by a whirlwind up into heaven. Elijah and Elisha were at Gilgal. [2]Elijah said to Elisha, "Please stay here. The Lord has told me to go to Bethel."

But Elisha said, "As the Lord lives, and as you live, I won't leave you." So they went down to Bethel. [3]A group of the prophets at Bethel came to Elisha. They said to him, "Do you know the Lord will take your master away from you today?"

Elisha said, "Yes, I know. But don't talk about it."

[4]Elijah said to him, "Stay here, because the Lord has sent me to Jericho."

But Elisha said, "As the Lord lives, and as you live, I won't leave you."

So they went to Jericho. [5]A group of the prophets at Jericho came to Elisha. They said, "Do you know that the Lord will take your master away from you today?"

Elisha answered, "Yes, I know. But don't talk about it."

⁶Elijah said to Elisha, "Stay here. The Lord has sent me to the Jordan River."

Elisha answered, "As the Lord lives, and as you live, I won't leave you."

So the two of them went on. ⁷Fifty men from a group of the prophets came. They stood far from where Elijah and Elisha were by the Jordan. ⁸Elijah took off his coat. Then he rolled it up and hit the water. The water divided to the right and to the left. Then Elijah and Elisha crossed over on dry ground.

⁹After they had crossed over, Elijah said to Elisha, "What can I do for you before I am taken from you?"

Elisha said, "Leave me a double share of your spirit."

¹⁰Elijah said, "You have asked a hard thing. But if you see me when I am taken from you, it will be yours. If you don't, it won't happen."

¹¹Elijah and Elisha were still walking and talking. Then a chariot and horses of fire appeared. The chariot and horses of fire separated Elijah from Elisha. Then Elijah  went up to heaven in a whirlwind. ¹²Elisha saw it and shouted, "My father! My father! The chariots

of Israel and their horsemen!" Elisha did not see him anymore. Elisha grabbed his own clothes and tore them to show how sad he was.

[13]He picked up Elijah's coat that had fallen from him. Then Elisha returned and stood on the bank of the Jordan. [14]Elisha hit the water with Elijah's coat. He said, "Where is the Lord, the God of Elijah?" When he hit the water, it divided to the right and to the left. Then Elisha crossed over.

[15a]A group of the prophets at Jericho were watching. They said, "Elisha now has the spirit Elijah had." They came to meet him. [16a]They said to him, "There are 50 strong men with us! Please let them go and look for your master."

[17b]So they sent 50 men who looked for three days. But they could not find Elijah.

A Room for Elisha

(From 2 Kings 4)

4:[8]One day Elisha went to Shunem. An important woman lived there. She begged Elisha to stay and eat. So every time Elisha passed by, he stopped there to eat. [9]The woman said to her husband, "I know that Elisha is a holy man of God. He passes by our house all the time. [10]Let's make a small room on the roof. Let's put a bed in the room for Elisha. . . . Then when he comes by, he can stay there."

[11]One day Elisha came to the woman's house. He went to his room and rested. [12a]He said to his ser-

vant Gehazi, ¹⁴" . . . What can we do for her [the Shunammite woman]?"

Gehazi answered, "She has no son, and her husband is old."

¹⁵Then Elisha said, "Call her." So he [Gehazi] called her, and she stood in the doorway. ¹⁶Then Elisha said, "About this time next year, you will hold a son in your arms."

The woman said, "No, master, man of God. Don't lie to me!"

¹⁷But the woman became pregnant. And she gave birth to a son at that time the next year as Elisha had told her.

¹⁸The child grew. One day he went out to his father, who was with the men harvesting grain. ¹⁹The boy said to his father, "My head! My head!"

The father said to his servant, "Carry him to his mother!" ²⁰The servant took him to his mother. He lay on his mother's lap until noon. Then he died. ²¹She took him up and laid him on Elisha's bed. Then she shut the door and went out.

²²She called to her husband. She said, "Send me one of the servants and one of the donkeys. Then I can go quickly to the man of God and come back."

²⁵ᵃSo she went to Elisha at Mount Carmel.

²⁸She said, "Master, I didn't tell you I wanted a son. I told you, 'Don't fool me.'"

²⁹Then Elisha said to Gehazi, "Get ready. Take my walking stick in your hand and go quickly. . . . Lay my walking stick on the face of the boy."

³¹Gehazi went on ahead. He laid the walking stick on the child's face. But the child did not talk or

move. Then Gehazi went back to meet Elisha. He told Elisha, "The child has not awakened."

³²Elisha came into the house. There was the child lying dead on his bed. ³³When Elisha entered the room, he shut the door. Only he and the child were in the room. Then Elisha prayed to the Lord. ³⁴He went to the bed and lay on the child. He put his mouth on the child's mouth. He put his eyes on the child's eyes and his hands on the child's hands. He stretched himself out on top of the child. Then the child's skin became warm. ³⁵Elisha turned away and walked around the room. . . . Then the child sneezed seven times and opened his eyes.

^{36b}Elisha said [to the Shunammite woman], "Pick up your son." ³⁷She came in and fell at Elisha's feet. She bowed facedown to the floor. Then she picked up her son and went out.

Naaman's Skin Disease

(From 2 Kings 5)

5:¹Naaman was commander of the army of the king of Aram. He was a great man to his master. He had much honor because the Lord had used him to give victory to Aram. He was a mighty and brave man. But he had a harmful skin disease.

²The Arameans had gone out to steal from the Israelites. And they had taken a little girl as a captive from Israel. This little girl served Naaman's wife. ³She said to her mistress, "I wish that my master would meet the prophet who lives in Samaria. He would heal Naaman of his disease."

⁴Naaman went to the king. He told him what the girl from Israel had said. ⁵The king of Aram said, "Go now. And I will send a letter to the king of Israel." So Naaman left and took about 750 pounds of silver. He also took about 150 pounds of gold and ten changes of clothes with him. ⁶He brought the letter to the king of Israel. It read, "I am sending my servant Naaman to you. I'm sending him so you can heal him of his skin disease."

⁷The king of Israel read the letter. Then he tore his clothes to show how upset he was. He said, "I'm not God! I can't kill and make alive again! Why does this man send someone with a harmful skin disease for me to heal? You can see that the king of Aram is trying to start trouble with me!"

⁸Elisha, the man of God, heard that the king of Israel had torn his clothes. So he sent a message to the king. It said, "Why have you become so upset that you tore your clothes? Let Naaman come to me. Then he will know there is a prophet in Israel!" ⁹So Naaman went with his horses and chariots to Elisha's house. And he stood outside the door.

¹⁰Elisha sent a messenger to Naaman. The messenger said, "Go and wash in the Jordan River seven times. Then your skin will be healed, and you will be clean."

¹¹Naaman became angry and left. He said, "I thought Elisha would surely come out and stand before me. I thought he would call on the name of the Lord his God. I thought he would wave his hand over the place and heal the disease! ¹²Abana and Pharpar, the rivers of Damascus, are better than all the waters of Israel! Why can't I wash in them and become clean?" So Naaman went away very angry.

¹³But Naaman's servants came near and talked to him. They said, "My father, if the prophet had told you to do some great thing, wouldn't you have done it? Doesn't it make more sense just to do it? After all, he only told you, 'Wash, and you will be clean.'" ¹⁴So Naaman went down and dipped in the Jordan seven times. He did just as Elisha had said. Then Naaman's skin became new again. It was like the skin of a little boy. And Naaman was clean!

Horses and Chariots of Fire

(From 2 Kings 6)

6:⁸The king of Aram was at war with Israel. He had a council meeting with his officers. He said, "I will set up my camp in this place."

⁹But Elisha sent a message to the king of Israel. It said, "Be careful! Don't pass that place. The Arameans are going down there!"

¹⁰The king of Israel checked the place about which Elisha had warned him. Elisha warned him several times. So the king added guards in those places.

¹¹The king of Aram was angry about this. He called his officers together. He said to them, "Tell me who of us is working for the king of Israel."

¹²One of the officers of the king of Aram said, "No, my master and king. It's Elisha, the prophet from Israel. He can tell you what you speak in your bedroom."

¹³The king said, "Go and find him. Then I can send men and catch him."

The servants came back and reported, "He is in Dothan."

¹⁴Then the king sent horses, chariots and a large army to Dothan. They arrived at night and surrounded the city.

¹⁵The servant of Elisha got up early. When he went out, he saw an army with horses and chariots all around the city. The servant said to Elisha, "Oh, my master, what can we do?"

¹⁶Elisha said, "Don't be afraid. The army that fights for us is larger than the one against us."

¹⁷Then Elisha prayed, "Lord, open my servant's eyes. Let him see."

The Lord opened the eyes of the young man. And he

saw that the mountain was full of horses and chariots of fire all around Elisha.

¹⁸As the enemy came down toward Elisha, he prayed to the Lord. He said, "Make these people blind." So the Lord made the Aramean army blind, as Elisha had asked.

¹⁹Elisha said to them, "This is not the right road. This is not the right city. Follow me. I'll take you to the man you are looking for." Then Elisha led them to Samaria.

²⁰After they entered Samaria, Elisha said, "Lord, open these men's eyes so they can see." So the Lord opened their eyes. And the Aramean army saw that they were inside the city of Samaria!

²¹The king of Israel saw the Aramean army. He said to Elisha, "My father, should I kill them? Should I kill them?"

²²Elisha answered, "Don't kill them. You wouldn't kill people whom you captured with your sword and bow. Give them food and water. And let them eat and drink. Then let them go home to their master." ²³So he prepared a great feast for the Aramean army. They ate and drank. Then the king sent them away. They went home to their master. The soldiers of Aram did not come anymore into the land of Israel.

Hezekiah Prays for God's Help

(From 2 Kings 19 and 20)

19:⁹The king [of Assyria] . . . sent messengers to Hezekiah. The king said: ¹⁰"Say this to Hezekiah king of Judah: Don't be fooled by the god you trust. Don't believe him when he says Jerusalem will not be defeated by the king of Assyria. ¹¹You have heard what the kings of Assyria have done. They have completely defeated every country. Do not think you will be saved."

¹⁴Hezekiah received the letter from the messengers and read it. Then he went up to the Temple of the Lord. Hezekiah spread the letter out before the Lord. ¹⁵And he prayed to the Lord: "Lord, God of Israel, your throne is between the gold creatures with wings! Only you are God of all the kingdoms of the earth. You made the heavens and the earth. ¹⁶Hear, Lord, and listen. Open your eyes, Lord, and see. Listen to the word Sennacherib has said to insult the living God. ¹⁷It is true, Lord. The kings of Assyria have destroyed these countries and their lands.¹⁹Now, Lord our God, save us from the king's power. Then all the kingdoms of the earth will know that you, Lord, are the only God."

³⁵That night the angel of the Lord went out. He killed 185,000 men in the Assyrian camp. The people got up early the next morning. And they saw all the dead bodies! ³⁶So Sennacherib king of Assyria left. He went back to Nineveh and stayed there.

20:¹At that time Hezekiah became very sick. He was almost dead. The prophet Isaiah son of Amoz went to see him. Isaiah told him, "This is what the Lord says: You are going to die. So you should give your last orders to everyone. You will not get well."

²Hezekiah turned toward the wall and prayed to the Lord. He said, ³"Lord, please remember that I have always obeyed you. I have given myself completely to you. I have done what you said was right." And Hezekiah cried loudly.

⁴Before Isaiah had left the middle courtyard, the Lord spoke his word to Isaiah: ⁵"Go back and tell Hezekiah, the leader of my people: 'This is what the Lord, the God of your ancestor David, says: I have heard your prayer. And I have seen your tears. So I will heal you. Three days from now you will go up to the Temple of the Lord. ⁶ᵃI will add 15 years to your life.'"

⁸ᵃHezekiah asked Isaiah, "What will be the sign that the Lord will heal me?"

⁹Isaiah said, "The Lord will do what he says. This is the sign from the Lord to show you: Do you want the shadow to go forward ten steps? Or do you want it to go back ten steps?"

¹⁰Hezekiah answered, "It's easy for the shadow to go forward ten steps. Instead, let it go back ten steps."

¹¹Then Isaiah the prophet called to the Lord. And the Lord brought the shadow back ten steps. It went back up the stairway of Ahaz that it had gone down.

The Boy King Joash Repairs the Temple

(From 2 Chronicles 24)

24:¹Joash was seven years old when he became king. And he ruled 40 years in Jerusalem. His mother's name was Zibiah. She was from Beersheba. ²Joash did what the Lord said was right as long as Jehoiada the priest was alive. ³Jehoiada chose two wives for Joash. And Joash had sons and daughters.

⁴Later, Joash decided to repair the Temple of the Lord. ⁵He called the priests and the Levites together. He said to them, "Go to the towns of Judah. Gather the money all the Israelites have to pay every year. Use it to repair the Temple of your God. Do this now." But the Levites did not hurry.

⁶So King Joash called Jehoiada the leading priest. Joash said to him, "Why haven't you made the Levites bring in the tax money from Judah and Jerusalem? Moses the Lord's servant and the people of Israel used that money for the Holy Tent."

⁷In the past the sons of wicked Athaliah had broken into the Temple of God. They had used its holy things for worshiping the Baal idols.

⁸King Joash commanded that a box for contributions be made. It was to be put outside, at the gate of the Temple of the Lord. ⁹Then the Levites made an announcement in Judah and Jerusalem. They told the people to bring the tax money to the Lord. Moses the servant of God had made the Israelites give it while they were in the desert. ¹⁰All the officers and

people were happy to give their money. They put it in the box until the box was full. ¹¹Then the Levites would take the box to the king's officers. They would see that it was full of money. Then the king's royal assistant and the leading priest's officer would come and take out the money. Then they would take the box back to its place. They did this often and gathered much money. ¹²King Joash and Jehoiada gave the money to the people who worked on the Temple of the Lord. And they hired stoneworkers and carpenters to repair the Temple of the Lord. They also hired people to work with iron and bronze to repair the Temple.

¹³The people worked hard. And the work to repair the Temple went well. They rebuilt the Temple of God to be as it was before. And they made it stronger. ¹⁴When the workers finished, they brought the money that was left to King Joash and Jehoiada. They used that money to make things for the Temple of the Lord. They made things for the service in the Temple and for the burnt offerings. They also made bowls and other things from gold and silver. Burnt offerings were given every day in the Temple of the Lord while Jehoiada was alive.

¹⁵Jehoiada grew old. . . . Then he died when he was 130 years old. ¹⁶Jehoiada was buried in

Jerusalem with the kings. He was buried there because he had done much good in Israel for God and his Temple.

Josiah Becomes King

(From 2 Chronicles 34 and 35)

34:¹Josiah was eight years old when he became king. He ruled 31 years in Jerusalem. ²He did what the Lord said was right. He did good things as his ancestor David had done. Josiah did not stop doing what was right.

³In his eighth year as king, Josiah began to obey the God his ancestor David had followed. This was while Josiah was still young. In his twelfth year as king, Josiah began to remove the false gods from Judah and Jerusalem. He destroyed the places for worshiping false gods. He removed the Asherah idols and the wooden and metal idols.

⁸In Josiah's eighteenth year as king, he made Judah and the Temple pure again. He sent Shaphan . . . , Maaseiah . . . and Joah . . . to repair the Temple of the Lord, the God of Josiah.

¹⁴ᵇAs they were doing this, Hilkiah the priest found the Book of the Lord's Teachings. These teachings had been given through Moses.

¹⁶ᵃThen Shaphan took the book to the king.

¹⁹The king heard the words of the Teachings. Then he tore his clothes to show how upset he was.

²⁹Then the king gathered all the older leaders of Judah and Jerusalem together. ³⁰He went up to

the Temple of the Lord. All the men from Judah and the people from Jerusalem went with him. . . . He read to them all the words in the Book of the Agreement. That book was found in the Temple of the Lord. [31]Then the king stood by his pillar. He made an agreement in the presence of the Lord. He agreed to follow the Lord and to obey his commands, rules and laws with his whole being. . . . [32]Then Josiah made all the people in Jerusalem and Benjamin promise to accept the agreement. The people of Jerusalem obeyed the agreement of God, the God their ancestors obeyed.

[33]And Josiah threw out the hateful idols from all the land that belonged to the Israelites. He led everyone in Israel to serve the Lord their God. While Josiah lived, the people obeyed the Lord, the God their ancestors obeyed.

35:[20b]After this, King Neco of Egypt led an army to attack Carchemish. It was a town on the Euphrates River. And Josiah marched out to fight against Neco. [21]But Neco sent messengers to Josiah. They said, "King Josiah, there should not be war between us. I did not come to fight you, but my enemies. God told me to hurry, and he is on my side. So don't fight God, or he will destroy you."

[22]But Josiah did not go away. He wore different clothes so no one would know who he was. He

refused to listen to what Neco said at God's command. So Josiah went to fight on the plain of Megiddo. ²³In the battle King Josiah was shot by arrows. He told his servants, "Take me away. I am badly wounded." ²⁴ᵃSo they took him out of his chariot. And they put him in another chariot he had brought to the battle. Then they took him to Jerusalem where he died.

The Fall of Jerusalem
(From 2 Chronicles 36)

36:¹The people of Judah chose Josiah's son Jehoahaz. They made him king in Jerusalem in his father's place.

²Jehoahaz was 23 years old when he became king. And he was king in Jerusalem for three months. ³ᵃThen King Neco of Egypt made Jehoahaz no longer a king in Jerusalem. ⁴ᵃThe king of Egypt made Jehoahaz's brother Eliakim the king of Judah and Jerusalem. Then Neco changed Eliakim's name to Jehoiakim.

⁵Jehoiakim was 25 years old when he became king. And he was king in Jerusalem for 11 years. He did what the Lord his God said was wrong. ⁶King Nebuchadnezzar of Babylon attacked Judah. He captured Jehoiakim and put bronze chains on him. Then Nebuchadnezzar took him to Babylon. ⁷Nebuchadnezzar took some of the things from the Temple of the Lord. And he took them to Babylon and put them in his own palace.

⁸ᵇJehoiakim's son Jehoiachin became king in his place.

⁹ᵃJehoiachin was 18 years old when he became king of Judah. And he was king in Jerusalem for three months and ten days. He did what the Lord said was wrong. ¹⁰In the spring King Nebuchadnezzar sent some servants to get Jehoiachin. They took him and some valuable treasures from the Temple of the Lord to Babylon. Then Nebuchadnezzar made Jehoiachin's relative Zedekiah the king of Judah and Jerusalem.

¹¹Zedekiah was 21 years old when he became king of Judah. And he was king in Jerusalem for 11 years. ¹²ᵃZedekiah did what the Lord his God said was wrong.

¹⁵The Lord, the God of their ancestors, sent prophets again and again to warn his people. He did this because he had pity for them and for his Temple. ¹⁶But they made fun of God's prophets. They hated God's messages. So they refused to listen to the prophets. Finally God became so angry with his people that he could not be stopped. ¹⁷So God brought the king of Babylon to attack them. . . . He [the king of Babylon] did not have mercy on the people. . . . ¹⁸Nebuchadnezzar carried away to Babylon all the things from the Temple of God, both large and small. He took all the treasures from the Temple of the Lord and from the king and his officers. ¹⁹Nebuchadnezzar and his army set fire to God's Temple. They broke down Jerusalem's wall. And they burned all the palaces. They took or destroyed every valuable thing in Jerusalem.

²⁰Nebuchadnezzar took captive to Babylon the

people who were left alive. And he forced them to be slaves for him and his descendants. They remained there as slaves until the Persian kingdom defeated Babylon.

²²ᵃIt was the first year Cyrus was king of Persia. The Lord caused Cyrus to write an announcement and send it everywhere in his kingdom.

²³This is what Cyrus king of Persia says:

"The Lord, the God of heaven, has given all the kingdoms of the earth to me. And he has appointed me to build a Temple for him at Jerusalem in Judah. Now all of you who are God's people are free to go to Jerusalem. May the Lord your God be with you."

Nehemiah Rebuilds the Walls

(From Nehemiah 1 and 2)

1:¹ᵇI, Nehemiah, was in the capital city of Susa. It was in the month of Kislev. This was in the twentieth year. ²One of my brothers named Hanani came from Judah. Some other men were with him. I asked them about the Jews who lived through the captivity. And I also asked about Jerusalem.

³They answered, "Nehemiah, those who are left from the captivity are back in the area of Judah.

But they are in much trouble and are full of shame. The wall around Jerusalem is broken down. And its gates have been burned."

⁴ᵃWhen I heard these things, I sat down and cried for several days.

2:¹ᵇIt was in the twentieth year King Artaxerxes was king. He wanted some wine. So I took some and gave it to the king. I had not been sad in his presence before. ²So the king said, "Why does your face look sad? You are not sick. Your heart must be sad."

Then I was very afraid. ³I said to the king, "May the king live forever! My face is sad because the city where my ancestors are buried lies in ruins. And its gates have been destroyed by fire."

⁴Then the king said to me, "What do you want?"

First I prayed to the God of heaven. ⁵Then I answered the king, "Send me to the city in Judah where my ancestors are buried. I will rebuild it. Do this if you are willing and if I have pleased you."

⁶ᵇHe asked me, "How long will your trip take? When will you get back?" It pleased the king to send me. So I set a time.

⁷I also said to him, "If you are willing, give me letters for the governors west of the Euphrates River. Tell them to let me pass safely through their lands on my way to Judah." ⁸ᵇSo the king gave me the letters. This was because God was showing kindness to me. ⁹So I went to the governors west of the Euphrates River. I gave them the king's letters. The king had also sent army officers and soldiers on horses with me.

¹¹I went to Jerusalem and stayed there three days. ¹²ᵃThen at night I started out with a few men. ¹³ᵇI was inspecting the walls of Jerusalem. They had been broken down. And the gates had been destroyed by fire. ¹⁶The officers did not know where I had gone or what I was doing. I had not yet said anything to the Jews, the priests, the important men or the officers. I had not said anything to any of the others who would do the work.

¹⁷Then I said to them, "You can see the trouble we have here. Jerusalem is a pile of ruins. And its gates have been burned. Come, let's rebuild the wall of Jerusalem. Then we won't be full of shame any longer." ¹⁸I also told them how God had been kind to me. And I told them what the king had said to me.

Then they answered, "Let's start rebuilding." So they began to work hard.

Esther Becomes Queen

(From Esther 1 and 2)

1:¹ This is what happened during the time of King Xerxes. He was the king who ruled the 127 areas from India to Cush. ²In those days King Xerxes ruled from his capital city of Susa. ³ᵃIn the third year of his rule, he gave a banquet. It was for all his important men and royal officers.

⁹Queen Vashti also gave a banquet. It was for the women in the royal palace of King Xerxes.

¹⁰ᵃOn the seventh day of the banquet, King Xerxes . . . gave a command to the seven [men] who served him. ¹¹ᵃHe commanded them to bring him Queen Vashti, wearing her royal crown. She was to come to show her beauty to the people and important men. ¹²The [servants] told Queen Vashti about the king's command. But she refused to come. Then the king became very angry.

¹⁵The king asked [his wise men], "What does the law say must be done to Queen Vashti? She has not obeyed the command of King Xerxes, which the [servants] took to her."

¹⁶ᵃThen Memucan [a wise man] spoke to the king and the other important men. He said, ¹⁹" . . . Our king, if it pleases you, give a royal order. . . . The law should say Vashti is never again to enter the presence of King Xerxes. Also let the king give her place as queen to someone who is better than she is."

2:²Then the king's personal servants had a suggestion. They said, "Let a search be made for beautiful young [girls] for the king. ³ᵃLet the king choose supervisors in every area of his kingdom. Let them bring every beautiful young [girl] to the palace at Susa. ⁴Then let the girl who pleases the king most become queen in place of Vashti." The king liked this advice. So he did as they said.

⁵ᵃNow there was a Jewish man in the palace of Susa. His name was Mordecai. ⁷Mordecai had a

cousin named Hadassah, who had no father or mother. So Mordecai took care of her. Hadassah was also called Esther, and she had a very pretty figure and face. Mordecai had adopted her as his own daughter when her father and mother died.

⁸The king's command and order had been heard. And many girls had been brought to the palace in Susa. They had been put under the care of Hegai. When this happened, Esther was also taken to the king's palace. She was put into the care of Hegai, who was in charge of the women. ⁹Esther pleased Hegai, and he liked her. So Hegai quickly began giving Esther her beauty treatments and special food. He gave her seven servant girls chosen from the king's palace. Then Hegai moved Esther and her seven servant girls to the best part of the women's quarters.

¹⁵ᵇThe time came for Esther to go to the king. . . . ¹⁶ᵃSo Esther was taken to King Xerxes in the royal palace.

¹⁷And the king was pleased with Esther more than with any of the other girls. . . . So King Xerxes put a royal crown on Esther's head. And he made her queen in place of Vashti.

Haman Plots Against Mordecai

(From Esther 3—5)

3:¹After these things happened, King Xerxes honored Haman. . . . He gave him a new rank that was higher than all the important men. ²And all the royal officers at the king's gate would bow down and kneel before Haman. This was what the king had ordered. But Mordecai would not bow down, and he did not kneel.

⁵Then Haman saw that Mordecai would not bow down to him or kneel before him. And he became very angry. ⁶He had been told who the people of Mordecai were. . . . So he looked for a way to destroy all of Mordecai's people, the Jews, in all of Xerxes' kingdom.

¹³ᵃLetters were sent by messengers to all the king's empire. They stated the king's order to . . . completely wipe out all the Jews.

4:¹Now Mordecai heard about all that had been done. To show how upset he was, he tore his clothes. Then he put on rough cloth and ashes. And he went out into the city crying loudly and very sadly.

⁴ᵃEsther's servant girls . . . came to her and told her about Mordecai. Esther was very upset and afraid. ⁵Then Esther called for Hathach. He was one of the king's [servants]. . . . Esther ordered him to find out what was bothering Mordecai and why.

⁷ᵃThen Mordecai told Hathach everything that had happened to him. ⁸Mordecai also gave him a copy of the order to kill the Jews, which had been

given in Susa. . . . And Mordecai told him to order Esther to go into the king's presence. He wanted her to beg for mercy and to plead with him for her people.

¹⁰Then Esther told Hathach to say to Mordecai, ¹¹"All the royal officers and people of the royal areas know this: No man or woman may go to the king in the inner courtyard without being called. There is only one law about this. Anyone who enters must be put to death. But if the king holds out his gold scepter, that person may live. . . ."

¹²And Esther's message was given to Mordecai. ¹³Then Mordecai gave orders to say to Esther: "Just because you live in the king's palace, don't think that out of all the Jews you alone will escape. ¹⁴ᵇWho knows, you may have been chosen queen for just such a time as this."

¹⁵Then Esther sent this answer to Mordecai: ¹⁶"Go and get all the Jews in Susa together. For my sake, give up eating. Do not eat or drink for three days, night and day. I and my servant girls will also give up eating. Then I will go to the king, even though it is against the law. And if I die, I die."

¹⁷So Mordecai went away. He did everything Esther had told him to do.

5:¹On the third day Esther put on her royal robes. Then

she stood in the inner courtyard of the king's palace, facing the king's hall. The king was sitting on his royal throne in the hall, facing the doorway. [2]The king saw Queen Esther standing in the courtyard. When he saw her, he was very pleased. He held out to her the gold scepter that was in his hand. So Esther went up to him and touched the end of the scepter.

Esther Saves Her People

(From Esther 5 and 7)

5:[3]Then the king asked, "What is it, Queen Esther? What do you want to ask me? I will give you as much as half of my kingdom."

[4]Esther answered, "My king, if it pleases you, come today with Haman to a banquet. I have prepared it for him."

[5]Then the king said, "Bring Haman quickly so we may do what Esther asks."

So the king and Haman went to the banquet Esther had prepared for them. [6]As they were drinking wine, the king said to Esther, "Now, Esther, what are you asking for? I will give it to you. What is it you want? I will give you as much as half of my kingdom."

[7]Esther answered, "This is what I want and ask for. [8b]Come with Haman tomorrow to the banquet I will prepare for you. Then I will answer your question about what I want."

[9]Haman left the king's palace that day happy and content. Then he saw Mordecai at the king's gate.

And he saw that Mordecai did not stand up nor did he tremble with fear before him. So Haman became very angry with Mordecai.

¹⁴Then Haman's wife Zeresh and all his friends said, "Have a platform built to hang someone. Build it 75 feet high. And in the morning ask the king to have Mordecai hanged on it. Then go to the banquet with the king and be happy." Haman liked this suggestion. So he ordered the platform to be built.

7:¹So the king and Haman went in to eat with Queen Esther. ²ᵃThey were drinking wine. And the king said to Esther on this second day also, "What are you asking for? I will give it to you."

³Then Queen Esther answered, "My king, I hope you are pleased with me. If it pleases you, let me live. This is what I ask. And let my people live, too. This is what I want. ⁴ᵃI ask this because my people and I have been sold to be destroyed. We are to be killed and completely wiped out."

⁵Then King Xerxes asked Queen Esther, "Who is he? Where is he? Who has done such a thing?"

⁶Esther said, "A man who is against us! Our enemy is this wicked Haman!"

Then Haman was filled with terror before the king and queen. ⁷The king was very angry. He got up, left his wine and went out into the palace garden. But Haman stayed inside to beg Queen Esther to save his life. He could see that the king had already decided to kill him.

[9]Harbona was one of the [men] there serving the king. He said, "Look, a platform for hanging people stands near Haman's house. It is 75 feet high. This is the one Haman had prepared for Mordecai. . . ."

The king said, "Hang Haman on it!" [10]So they hanged Haman on the platform he had prepared for Mordecai. Then the king was not so angry anymore.

Psalms to Live By

THE LORD IS MY SHEPHERD

(From Psalm 23)

A Song of David.

[1]The Lord is my shepherd.
   I have everything I need.
[2]He gives me rest in green pastures.
   He leads me to calm water.
[3]He gives me new strength.
For the good of his name,
   he leads me on paths
     that are right.

[4]Even if I walk
   through a very dark
     valley,
I will not be afraid
   because you are with me.
Your rod and your walking stick comfort me.

⁵You prepare a meal for me
   in front of my enemies.
You pour oil on my head.
   You give me more than I can hold.
⁶Surely your goodness and love will be with me
   all my life.
And I will live in the house of the Lord forever.

LORD, TEACH ME YOUR RULES
(From Psalm 119)

¹Happy are the people who live pure lives.
   They follow the Lord's teachings.
²Happy are the people who keep his rules.
   They ask him for help with their whole heart.
³They don't do what is wrong.
   They follow his ways.
⁴Lord, you gave your orders
   to be followed completely.
⁵I wish I were more loyal
   in meeting your demands.
⁶Then I would not be ashamed
   when I think of your commands.
⁷When I learned that your laws are fair,
   I praised you with an honest heart.
⁸I will meet your demands.
   So please don't ever leave me.

⁹How can a young person live a pure life?
   He can do it by obeying your word.

¹⁰With all my heart I try to obey you, God.
Don't let me break your commands.
¹¹I have taken your words to heart
so I would not sin against you.
¹²Lord, you should be praised.
Teach me your demands.
¹³My lips will tell about
all the laws you have spoken.
¹⁴I enjoy living by your rules
as people enjoy great riches.
¹⁵I think about your orders
and study your ways.
¹⁶I enjoy obeying your
demands.
And I will not forget your
word.

²⁰I want to study
your laws all the time.
²⁴Your rules give me pleasure.
They give me good advice.

The Wise Words of Solomon

(From Proverbs 1 and 3)

PROVERBS 1

¹These are the wise words of Solomon son of
David. Solomon was king of Israel.

²They teach wisdom and self-control.
They give understanding.

³They will teach you how to be wise and self-controlled.
 They will teach you what is honest and fair and right.
⁴They give the ability to think to those with little knowledge.
 They give knowledge and good sense to the young.
⁵Wise people should also listen to them and learn even more.
 Even smart people will find wise advice in these words.
⁶Then they will be able to understand wise words and stories.
 They will understand the words of wise men and their riddles.

⁷Knowledge begins with respect for the Lord.
 But foolish people hate wisdom and self-control.

⁸My child, listen to your father's teaching.
 And do not forget your mother's advice.
⁹Their teaching will beautify your life.
 It will be like flowers in your hair or a chain around your neck.
¹⁰My child, sinners will try to lead you into sin.
 But do not follow them.
¹⁵My child, do not go along with them.
 Do not do what they do.

PROVERBS 3

¹My child, do not forget my teaching.
 Keep my commands in mind.
²Then you will live a long time.
 And your life will be successful.

³Don't ever stop being kind and
   truthful.
  Let kindness and truth
     show in all you do.
  Write them down in
     your mind as if on
     a tablet.
⁴Then you will be respected
  and pleasing to both God and men.

⁵Trust the Lord with all your heart.
  Don't depend on your own understanding.
⁶Remember the Lord in everything you do.
  And he will give you success.

⁷Don't depend on your own wisdom.
  Respect the Lord and refuse to do wrong.
⁸Then your body will be healthy.
  And your bones will be strong.

A Child Will Be Born

(From Isaiah 9 and 11)

9:¹ªBut suddenly there will be no more gloom for
the land that suffered.

²Now those people live in darkness.
  But they will see a great light.
They live in a place that is very dark.
  But a light will shine on them.
³God, you will cause the nation to grow.
  You will make the people happy.

And they will show their happiness to you.
It will be like the joy during harvest time.
It will be like the joy of people
taking what they have won in war.
⁴Like the time you defeated Midian,
you will take away their heavy load.
You will take away the heavy pole from their
backs.
You will take away the rod the enemy uses to
punish your people.
⁶A child will be born to us.
God will give a son to us.
He will be responsible for leading the people.
His name will be Wonderful Counselor, Powerful
God,
Father Who Lives Forever, Prince of Peace.
⁷Power and peace will be
in his kingdom.
It will continue to grow.
He will rule as king on
David's throne
and over David's
kingdom.
He will make it strong,
by ruling with
goodness and fair judgment.
He will rule it forever and ever.
The Lord of heaven's armies will do this
because of his strong love for his people.

ISAIAH 11

¹A branch will grow
from a stump of a tree that was cut down.

So a new king will come
  from the family of Jesse.
²The Spirit of the Lord will rest upon that king.
  The Spirit gives him wisdom, understanding,
    guidance and power.
  And the Spirit teaches him to know and respect
    the Lord.
³This king will be glad to obey the Lord.
 He will not judge by the way things look.
  He will not judge by what people say.
⁴He will judge the poor honestly.
  He will be fair in his decisions for the poor
    people of the land.
At his command evil people will be punished.
  By his words the wicked will be put to death.
⁵Goodness and fairness will give him strength.
  They will be like a belt around his waist.

⁶Then wolves will live in peace with lambs.
  And leopards will lie down to rest with goats.
Calves, lions and young bulls
      will eat together.
And a little child
    will lead them.
⁷Cows and bears will
    eat together in
    peace.
Their young will lie
    down together.
Lions will eat hay as
    oxen do.
⁹They will not hurt or destroy each other
  on all my holy mountain.

The earth will be full of the knowledge of the
    Lord,
    as the sea is full of water.

¹⁰At that time the new king from the family of
Jesse will stand as a banner for the people. The
nations will come together around him. And the
place where he lives will be filled with glory.

God Chooses Jeremiah

(From Jeremiah 1)

1:¹These are the words of Jeremiah son of
Hilkiah. He belonged to the family of priests who
lived in the town of Anathoth. That town is in the
land that belongs to the tribe of Benjamin. ²The
Lord spoke his word to Jeremiah. This happened
during the thirteenth year that Josiah
son of Amon was
king of Judah.
³The Lord also
spoke to Jeremiah
while Jehoiakim
son of Josiah was
king of Judah. And
the Lord spoke to
Jeremiah during the

11 years and 5 months Zedekiah son of Josiah was
king of Judah. After that, the people who lived in
Jerusalem were taken away as captives out of
their country.

⁴The Lord spoke these words to me:
⁵"Before I made you in your mother's womb, I
    chose you.
  Before you were born, I set you apart for a
    special work.
  I appointed you as a prophet to the nations."

⁶Then I said, "But Lord God, I don't know how to speak. I am only a boy."

⁷But the Lord said to me, "Don't say, 'I am only a boy.' You must go everywhere that I send you. You must say everything I tell you to say. ⁸Don't be afraid of anyone, because I am with you. I will protect you," says the Lord.

⁹Then the Lord reached out with his hand and touched my mouth. He said to me, "See, I am putting my words in your mouth. ¹⁰Today I have put you in charge of nations and kingdoms. You will pull up and tear down, destroy and overthrow. You will build up and plant."

¹¹The Lord spoke this word to me: "Jeremiah, what do you see?"

I answered the Lord and said, "I see a stick of almond wood."

¹²The Lord said to me, "You have seen correctly! And I am watching to make sure my words come true."

¹³The Lord spoke his word to me again: "Jeremiah, what do you see?"

I answered the Lord and said, "I see a pot of boiling water. It is tipping over from the north!"

¹⁴The Lord said to me, "Disaster will come from the north. It will happen to all the people who live

in this country. ¹⁵In a short time I will call all of the people in the northern kingdoms," said the Lord.

"Those kings will come and set up their thrones
near the entrance of the gates of Jerusalem.
They will attack the city walls around Jerusalem.
They will attack all the cities in Judah."

The Prophet's Scroll

(From Jeremiah 36)

36:¹The Lord spoke his word to Jeremiah. This was during the fourth year that Jehoiakim son of Josiah was king of Judah. This was his message: ²"Jeremiah, get a scroll. Write on it all the words I have spoken to you about Israel and Judah and all the nations. Write everything I have spoken to you since Josiah was king until now. ³Maybe the family of Judah will hear what disasters I am planning to bring on them. And maybe they will stop doing wicked things. Then I would forgive them for the sins and the evil things they have done."

⁴So Jeremiah called for Baruch son of Neriah. Jeremiah spoke the messages the Lord had given him. And Baruch wrote those messages on the scroll. ⁵Then Jeremiah said to Baruch, "I cannot go to the Temple of the Lord. I must stay here. ^{6a}So I want you to go to the Temple of the Lord. . . . Read to all the people of Judah from the scroll. ^{7a}Perhaps they will ask the Lord to help them."

[9a]It was the ninth month of the fifth year that Jehoiakim son of Josiah was king. A special time to give up eating was announced. All the people of Jerusalem were supposed to give up eating to honor the Lord. [10a]At that time Baruch read the scroll that contained Jeremiah's words. Baruch read the scroll in the Temple of the Lord to all the people there.

[14]Then the officers sent a man named Jehudi son of Nethaniah to Baruch. . . . Jehudi said to Baruch, "Bring the scroll that you read to the people and come with me."

So Baruch son of Neriah took the scroll and went with Jehudi to the officers. [15]Then the officers said to Baruch, "Sit down and read the scroll to us."

So Baruch read the scroll to them. [16]When the officers heard all the words, they became afraid. And they looked at one another. They said to Baruch, "We must certainly tell the king about these words." [17]Then the officers asked Baruch, "Tell us, Baruch, where did you get these words you wrote on the scroll? Did you write down what Jeremiah said to you?"

[18]"Yes," Baruch answered. "Jeremiah spoke, and I wrote down all the words with ink on this scroll."

[19]Then the officers said to Baruch, "You and Jeremiah must go and hide. Don't tell anyone where you are hiding."

[20]Then the officers put the scroll in the room of Elishama the royal assistant. Then they went to the king in the courtyard and told him all about the scroll. [21a]So King Jehoiakim sent Jehudi to get the scroll. . . . Then Jehudi read the scroll to the

king. ^{22b}So King Jehoiakim was sitting in the winter apartment. There was a fire burning in a small firepot in front of him. ²³Jehudi began to read from the scroll. But after he had read three or four columns, the king cut

those columns off of the scroll with a pen knife. And he threw them into the firepot. Finally, the whole scroll was burned in the fire.

Jeremiah Is Rescued

(From Jeremiah 37 and 38)

37:¹Nebuchadnezzar was king of Babylon. He appointed Zedekiah son of Josiah as king of Judah. Zedekiah took the place of Jehoiachin son of Jehoiakim. ²But Zedekiah, his servants and the people of Judah did not listen to the words of the Lord. The Lord had spoken his words through Jeremiah the prophet.

¹⁷Then King Zedekiah sent for Jeremiah and had him brought to the palace. Zedekiah talked to Jeremiah in private. He asked Jeremiah, "Is there any message from the Lord?"

Jeremiah answered, "Yes, there is a message from the Lord. Zedekiah, you will be handed over to the king of Babylon."

38:¹Some of the officers heard what Jeremiah

was prophesying. . . . Jeremiah was telling all the people this message: [2]"This is what the Lord says: 'Everyone who stays in Jerusalem will die in war. Or he will die of hunger or terrible diseases. But everyone who surrenders to the Babylonian army will live. They will escape with their lives and live.' [3]And this is what the Lord says: 'This city of Jerusalem will surely be handed over to the army of the king of Babylon. He will capture this city!'"

[4]Then the officers said to the king, "Jeremiah must be put to death! He is making the soldiers who are still in the city become discouraged. He is discouraging everyone by the things he is saying. . . . He wants to ruin the people of Jerusalem."

[5]King Zedekiah said to them, "Jeremiah is in your control. I cannot do anything to stop you!"

[6]So the officers took Jeremiah and put him into the well of Malkijah, the king's son. . . . The officers used ropes to lower Jeremiah into the well. It did not have any water in it, only mud. And Jeremiah sank down into the mud.

[7]But Ebed-Melech heard that the officers had put Jeremiah into the well. Ebed-Melech was a Cushite, and he was a [servant] in the palace. King Zedekiah was sitting at the Benjamin Gate. [8]So Ebed-Melech left the palace and went to the king. Ebed-Melech said, [9]"My master and king, the

rulers have acted in an evil way. They have treated Jeremiah the prophet badly! They have thrown him into a well! They have left him there to die! When there is no more bread in the city, he will starve."

¹⁰Then King Zedekiah commanded Ebed-Melech the Cushite: "Ebed-Melech, take 30 men from the palace with you. Go and lift Jeremiah the prophet out of the well before he dies."

¹¹So Ebed-Melech took the men with him. And he went to a room under the storeroom in the palace. He took some old rags and worn-out clothes from that room. Then he let those rags down with some ropes to Jeremiah in the well. ¹²Ebed-Melech the Cushite said to Jeremiah, "Put these old rags and worn-out clothes under your arms. They will be pads for the ropes." So Jeremiah did as Ebed-Melech said. ¹³The men pulled Jeremiah up with the ropes and lifted him out of the well. And Jeremiah stayed under guard in the courtyard.

God Speaks to Ezekiel
(From Ezekiel 1—3)

1:¹It was the thirtieth year, on the fifth day of the fourth month of our captivity. I, Ezekiel, was by the Kebar River in Babylon. I was among the people who had been carried away as captives from the land of Judah. The sky opened, and I saw visions of God.

2:¹[God] said to me, "Human being, stand up on your feet. Then I will speak with you." ²While he spoke to me, the Spirit entered me and put me on my feet. Then I heard the Lord speaking to me.

³He said, "Human being, I am sending you to the people of Israel. They are a nation of people who turned against me. They broke away from me. They and their ancestors have sinned against me until this very day. ⁴And I am sending you to people who are stubborn. They do not obey. You will say this to them, 'This is what the Lord God says.' ⁵The people may listen, or they may not. They are a people who turn against me. But whatever they do, they will know that a prophet has been among them.

⁷"But speak my words to them. They may listen, or they may not, because they turn against me. ⁸But you, human being, listen to what I say to you. Don't turn against me as those people do. Open your mouth and eat what I am giving you."

⁹I looked and saw a hand stretched out to me. A scroll was in the hand. ¹⁰The Lord opened the scroll in front of me. The scroll was written on the front and back. Funeral songs, sad writings and troubles were written on the scroll.

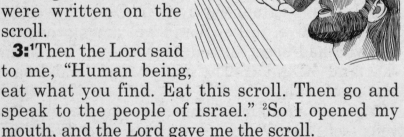

3:¹Then the Lord said to me, "Human being, eat what you find. Eat this scroll. Then go and speak to the people of Israel." ²So I opened my mouth, and the Lord gave me the scroll.

³The Lord said to me, "Human being, eat this scroll which I am giving you. Fill your stomach with it." Then I ate it. And it was sweet like honey in my mouth.

⁴Then the Lord said to me, "Human being, go to the people of Israel. Speak my words to them. ⁷But the people of Israel are not willing to listen to you. This is because they are not willing to listen to me. Yes, all the people of Israel are stubborn and will not obey. ⁸ᵃSee, I have made you as stubborn as they are. ⁹ᵇDon't be afraid of them. Don't be frightened by them. They are a people who turn against me."

¹⁰Also, the Lord said to me, "Human being, believe all the words that I will speak to you. And listen carefully. ¹¹Go to the captives, your people. And speak to them, whether they will listen or not. Tell them, 'The Lord God says this.'"

¹²Then the Spirit lifted me up. And I heard a loud rumbling sound behind me. A voice said, "Praise God in heaven." ¹⁴ᵇI felt the great power of the Lord.

Daniel Is Taken to Babylon
(From Daniel 1)

1:³Then King Nebuchadnezzar [of Babylon] gave an order to Ashpenaz, his chief officer. He told Ashpenaz to bring some of the [captive] Israelite men into his house. He wanted them to be from important families. And he wanted those who were from the family of the king of Judah. ⁴King

Nebuchadnezzar wanted only healthy, young, Israelite men. These men were not to have anything wrong with their bodies. They were to be handsome and well educated. They were to be able to learn and understand things. . . . ⁵The king gave the young men a certain amount of food and wine every day. That was the same kind of food that the king ate. They were to be trained for three years. Then the young men would become servants of the king of Babylon. ⁶Among those young men were some from the people of Judah. These were Daniel, Hananiah, Mishael and Azariah.

⁷Then Ashpenaz, the chief officer, gave them Babylonian names. Daniel's new name was Belteshazzar. Hananiah's was Shadrach. Mishael's was Meshach. And Azariah's new name was Abednego.

⁸Daniel decided not to eat the king's food and wine because that would make him unclean. So he asked Ashpenaz for permission not to make himself unclean in this way.

⁹God made Ashpenaz want to be kind and merciful to Daniel. ¹⁰But Ashpenaz said to Daniel, "I am afraid of my master, the king. He ordered me to give you this food and drink. If you don't eat this food, you will begin to look worse than other young men your age. The king will see this. And he will cut off my head because of you."

¹¹Ashpenaz had ordered a guard to watch Daniel, Hananiah, Mishael and Azariah. ¹²Daniel said to the

guard, "Please give us this test for ten days: Don't give us anything but vegetables to eat and water to drink. [13]Then after ten days compare us with the other young men who eat the king's food. See for yourself who looks healthier. Then you judge for yourself how you want to treat us, your servants."

[14]So the guard agreed to test them for ten days. [15]After ten days they looked very healthy. They looked better than all of the young men who ate the king's food. [16]So the guard took away the king's special food and wine. He gave Daniel, Hananiah, Mishael and Azariah vegetables instead.

[17]God gave these four men wisdom and the ability to learn. They learned many kinds of things people had written and studied. Daniel could also understand all kinds of visions and dreams.

[18]The end of the three years came. And Ashpenaz brought all of the young men to King Nebuchadnezzar. [19]The king talked to them. He found that none of the young men were as good as Daniel, Hananiah, Mishael and Azariah. So those four young men became the king's servants. [20]Every time the king asked them about something important, they showed much wisdom and understanding. He found they were ten times better than all the fortune-tellers and magicians in his kingdom.

The Blazing Furnace
(From Daniel 3)

3:[1a]Now King Nebuchadnezzar had a gold statue made. [2]Then the king called the important leaders. . . . He wanted these men to come to the special service for the statue he had set up. [4]Then the man who made announcements for the king spoke in a loud voice. He said, " . . . This is what you are commanded to do: [5]You will hear the sound of the horns, flutes, lyres, zithers, harps, pipes and all the other musical instruments. When this happens, you must bow down and worship the gold statue. . . . [6b]Anyone who doesn't will be quickly thrown into a blazing furnace."

[7] . . . So they bowed down and worshiped the gold statue that King Nebuchadnezzar had set up.

[8a]Then some Babylonians came up to the king. [9a]They said to King Nebuchadnezzar, " . . . [10]Our king, you gave a command. You said that everyone . . . would have to bow down and worship the gold statue. [12]Our king, there are some men of Judah who did not pay attention to your order. . . . Their names are Shadrach, Meshach and Abednego. They do not serve your gods. And they do not worship the gold statue you have set up."

[13a]Nebuchadnezzar became very angry. He called for Shadrach, Meshach and Abednego. [14]And Nebuchadnezzar said, " . . . Is it true that you do not serve my gods? And is it true that you did not worship the gold statue I have set up? [15]Now . . . you must be ready to bow down and worship the statue I made. . . . But if you do not worship it, you will be thrown quickly into the blazing furnace. . . . "

[16a]Shadrach, Meshach and Abednego answered the king. They said, [17a]"You can throw us into the blazing furnace. The God we serve is able to save us from the furnace and your power. [18]But even if

164

God does not save us, we want you, our king, to know this: We will not serve your gods. We will not worship the gold statue you have set up."

[19]Then Nebuchadnezzar was furious with Shadrach, Meshach and Abednego. He ordered the furnace to be heated seven times hotter than usual.

[21]So Shadrach, Meshach and Abednego were tied up and thrown into the blazing furnace. They were still wearing their robes, trousers, turbans and other clothes. [22b]The fire was so hot that the flames killed the strong soldiers who took Shadrach, Meshach and Abednego there. [23]Firmly tied, Shadrach, Meshach and Abednego fell into the blazing furnace.

[25]The king said, "Look! I see four men. They are walking around in the fire. They are not tied up, and they are not burned. The fourth man looks like a son of the gods."

[26]Then Nebuchadnezzar went to the opening of the blazing furnace. He shouted, "Shadrach, Meshach and Abednego, come out! Servants of the Most High God, come here!"

So Shadrach, Meshach and Abednego came out of the fire. [27]When they came out, . . . the fire had not harmed their bodies. Their hair was not burned. Their robes were not burned. And they didn't even smell like smoke.

^{28a}Then Nebuchadnezzar said, "Praise the God of Shadrach, Meshach and Abednego. Their God has sent his angel and saved his servants from the fire!"

Writing on the Wall
(From Daniel 5 and 6)

5:¹King Belshazzar gave a big banquet for 1,000 royal guests. And he drank wine with them. ^{2a}As Belshazzar was drinking his wine, he gave an order to his servants. He told them to bring the gold and silver cups that his ancestor Nebuchadnezzar had taken from the Temple in Jerusalem. ³So they brought the gold cups. . . . And the king and his royal guests, his wives and his slave women drank from them. ⁴As they were drinking, they praised their gods. These gods were made from gold, silver, bronze, iron, wood and stone.

⁵Then suddenly a person's hand appeared. The fingers wrote words on the plaster on the wall. This was near the lampstand in the royal palace. The king watched the hand as it wrote.

⁶King Belshazzar was very frightened. His face turned white, and his knees knocked together. He could not stand up because his legs were too weak.

⁸So all the king's wise men came in. But they could not read the writing. And they could not tell the king what it meant.

¹³So they brought Daniel to the king. The king

said to him, "Is your name Daniel? Are you one of the captives my father the king brought from Judah? [16]I have heard that you are able to explain what things mean. And you can find the answers to hard problems. Read this writing on the wall and explain it to me. If you can, I will give you purple clothes fit for a king. And I will put a gold chain around your neck. And you will become the third highest ruler in the kingdom."

[17]Then Daniel answered the king, "You may keep your gifts for yourself. Or you may give those rewards to someone else. I will read the writing on the wall for you. And I will explain to you what it means.

[25]"These are the words that were written on the wall: 'Mene, mene, tekel, parsin.'

[26]"This is what these words mean: Mene: God has counted the days until your kingdom will end. [27]Tekel: You have been weighed on the scales and found not good enough. [28]Parsin: Your kingdom is being divided. It will be given to the Medes and the Persians."

[29]Then Belshazzar gave an order for Daniel to be dressed in purple clothes. A gold chain was put around his neck. And he was announced to be the third highest ruler in the kingdom. [30]That very same night Belshazzar, king of the Babylonian people, was killed. [31]A man named Darius the

Mede became the new king. Darius was 62 years old.

6:¹Darius thought it would be a good idea to choose 120 governors. They would rule through all of his kingdom. ²And he chose three men as supervisors over those 120 governors. Daniel was one of these three supervisors. The king set up these men so that he would not be cheated. ³Daniel showed that he could do the work better than the other supervisors and the governors. Because of this, the king planned to put Daniel in charge of the whole kingdom.

Daniel and the Lions' Den
(From Daniel 6)

6:⁴ᵃSo the other supervisors and the governors tried to find reasons to accuse Daniel. But he went on doing the business of the government. And they could not find anything wrong with him. So they could not accuse him of doing anything wrong.

⁶So the supervisors and the governors went as a group to the king. They said: "King Darius, live forever! ⁷ᵇWe think the king should make this law that everyone would have to obey: No one should pray to any god or man except to you, our king. . . . Anyone who doesn't obey will be thrown into the lions' den. ⁸ᵃNow, our king, make the law. Write it down so it cannot be changed." ⁹So King Darius made the law and had it written.

¹⁰When Daniel heard that the new law had been

written, he went to his house. He went to his upstairs room. The windows of that room opened toward Jerusalem. Three times each day Daniel got down on his knees and prayed. He prayed and thanked God, just as he always had done.

[11]Then those men went as a group and found Daniel. They saw him praying and asking God for help. [12]So they went to the king. . . . They said, "Didn't you write a law that says no one may pray to any god or man except you, our king? Doesn't it say that anyone who disobeys . . . will be thrown into the lions' den?"

The king answered, "Yes, I wrote that law. And the laws of the Medes and Persians cannot be canceled."

[13]Then those men spoke to the king. They said, "Daniel is . . . not paying attention to the law you wrote. Daniel still prays to his God three times every day." [14a]The king became very upset when he heard this.

[15]Then those men went as a group to the king. They said, "Remember, our king, the law of the Medes and Persians. It says that no law or command given by the king can be changed."

[16]So King Darius gave the order. They brought Daniel and threw him into the lions' den. The king said to Daniel, "May the God you serve all the time save you!" [17a]A big stone was brought. It was put over the opening of the lions' den. [18]Then King Darius went back to his palace. He did not eat that night. . . . And he could not sleep.

[19]The next morning King Darius got up at dawn. He hurried to the lions' den. [20]As he came near the

den, he was worried. He called out to Daniel. He said, "Daniel, servant of the living God! Has your God that you always worship been able to save you from the lions?"

²¹Daniel answered, "My king, live forever! ²²My God sent his angel to close the lions' mouths. They have not hurt me, because my God knows I am innocent. I never did anything wrong to you, my king."

²³King Darius was very happy. He told his servants to lift Daniel out of the lions' den. So they lifted him out and did not find any injury on him. This was because Daniel had trusted in his God.

Jonah Runs from God

(From Jonah 1 and 2)

1:¹ The Lord spoke his word to Jonah son of Amittai: ²"Get up, go to the great city of Nineveh and preach against it. I see the evil things they do."

³But Jonah got up to run away from the Lord. He went to the city of Joppa. There he found a ship that was going to the city of Tarshish. Jonah paid for the trip and went aboard. He wanted to go to Tarshish to run away from the Lord.

⁴But the Lord sent a great wind on the sea. This wind made the sea very rough. So the ship was in danger of breaking apart. ⁵The sailors were afraid. Each man cried to his own god. The men began throwing the cargo into the sea. This would make the ship lighter so it would not sink.

But Jonah had gone down into the ship to lie down. He fell fast asleep. ⁶The captain of the ship came and said, "Why are you sleeping? Get up! Pray to your god! Maybe your god will pay attention to us. Maybe he will save us!"

⁷Then the men said to each other, "Let's throw lots to see who caused these troubles to happen to us."

So the men threw lots. The lot showed that the trouble had happened because of Jonah.

¹²Jonah said to them, "Pick me up, and throw me into the sea. Then it will calm down. I know it is my fault that this great storm has come on you."

¹⁴So the men cried to the Lord, "Lord, please don't let us die because of taking this man's life. Please don't think we are guilty of killing an innocent man. Lord, you have caused all this to happen. You wanted it this way." ¹⁵Then the men picked up Jonah and threw him into the sea. So the sea became calm. ¹⁶Then they began to fear the Lord very much. They offered a sacrifice to the Lord. They also made promises to him.

¹⁷And the Lord caused a very big fish to swallow Jonah. Jonah was in the stomach of the fish three days and three nights.

2:¹While Jonah was in the stomach of the fish, he prayed to the Lord his God. Jonah said,

²"I was in danger.
　So I called to the
　　Lord,
　and he answered
　　me.
I was about to die.
　So I cried to you,
　and you heard my voice.
³You threw me into the sea.
　I went down, down into the deep sea.
The water was all around me.
　Your powerful waves flowed over me.
⁶ᵇBut you saved me from death,
　Lord my God.

⁹"Lord, I will praise and thank you
　while I give sacrifices to you.
I will make promises to you.
　And I will do what I promise.
Salvation comes from the Lord!"

¹⁰Then the Lord spoke to the fish. And the fish spit Jonah out of its stomach onto the dry land.

Jonah Obeys God

(From Jonah 3 and 4)

3:¹Then the Lord spoke his word to Jonah again. The Lord said, ²"Get up. Go to the great city Nineveh. Preach against it what I tell you."
³So Jonah obeyed the Lord. He got up and went to

Nineveh. It was a very large city. It took a person three days just to walk across it. ⁴Jonah entered the city. . . . He preached to the people. He said, "After 40 days, Nineveh will be destroyed!"

⁵The people of Nineveh believed in God. They announced they would stop eating for a while. They put on rough cloth to show how sad they were. All the people in the city wore the cloth. People from the most important to the least important did this.

⁶When the king of Nineveh heard this news, he got up from his throne. He took off his robe. He covered himself with rough cloth and sat in ashes to show how upset he was.

¹⁰God saw what the people did. He saw that they stopped doing evil things. So God changed his mind and did not do what he had warned. He did not punish them.

4:¹But Jonah was very unhappy that God did not destroy the city. He was angry. ²He complained to the Lord and said, "I knew this would happen. I knew it when I was still in my own country. It is why I quickly ran away to Tarshish. I knew that you are a God who is kind and shows mercy. You don't become angry quickly. You have great love. I knew that you would rather forgive than punish them."

⁴Then the Lord said, "Do you think it is right for you to be angry?"

[5]Jonah went out and sat down east of the city. . . . He was waiting to see what would happen to the city. [6]The Lord made a plant grow quickly up over Jonah. This made a cool place for him to sit. And it helped him to be more comfortable. Jonah was very pleased to have the plant for shade. [7]The next day the sun rose. And God sent a worm to attack the plant. Then the plant died.

[8]When the sun was high in the sky, God sent a hot east wind to blow. The sun became very hot on Jonah's head. And he became very weak. He wished he were dead. Jonah said, "It is better for me to die than to live."

[9]But God said this to Jonah: "Do you think it is right for you to be angry because of the plant?"

Jonah answered, "It is right for me to be angry! I will stay angry until I die!"

[10]And the Lord said, "You showed concern for that plant. But you did not plant it or make it grow. It appeared in the night, and the next day it died. [11]Then surely I can show concern for the great city Nineveh. . . . There are more than 120,000 people living there. Those people simply do not know right from wrong!"

NEW TESTAMENT

About the Gospels—the Stories of Jesus' Life and Work

The first four books of the New Testament—Matthew, Mark, Luke, and John—are known as the Gospels, a word that means "good news." These books tell about the life and work of Jesus Christ.

Matthew, Mark, Luke, and John are not the same as biographies. A biography is a true story about a person's life that tells about most of the things that happened in his or her life. But the Gospels talk about only a part of Jesus' life—the two to three years of his work when he was in his early thirties. The Gospels only tell us parts of Jesus' early years—for example, his birth in Bethlehem, the visit of the wise men, the family's escape to Egypt, Jesus' visit to the Temple as a young boy.

The Gospels were written to tell us who Jesus is and to encourage us to believe and trust in him. The Gospels contain many facts about Jesus. But they are told to us by the Gospel writers to show that Jesus is the Son of God and the Savior of the world.

The Gospel writers often record the same event in the life of Jesus (for example, the feeding of five thousand people). But each Gospel also contains information about Jesus that is not found in any other Gospel. This is why we need all four Gospels. Together, they give us a clear picture of who Jesus is and what he did during his work here on earth.

In the next few pages you will find stories from all four of the Gospel books. These stories are in the order you would find them in your Bible. They start with Matthew's stories, move to Mark's, then Luke's, then John's. God had each Gospel writer tell particular stories that help us learn different things about Jesus, God's Son.

If you want to read these same stories in the order in which they happened, follow the list below.

Wise Men from the East

(From Matthew 1 and 2)

1:[18]The mother of Jesus Christ was Mary. And this is how the birth of Jesus came about. Mary was engaged to marry Joseph. But before they married, she learned she was going to have a baby. She was pregnant by the power of the Holy Spirit.

[20b]An angel of the Lord came to [Joseph] in a dream. The angel said, "Joseph, descendant of David, don't be afraid to take Mary as your wife. The baby in her is from the Holy Spirit. [21]She will give birth to a son. You will name the son Jesus. Give him that name because he will save his people from their sins."

[24]When Joseph woke up, he did what the Lord's angel had told him to do. Joseph married Mary.

2:[1]Jesus was born in the town of Bethlehem in Judea during the time when Herod was king. After Jesus was born, some wise men from the east came to Jerusalem. [2]They asked, "Where is the baby who was born to be the king of the Jews? We saw his star in the east. We came to worship him."

[3]When King Herod heard about this new king of the Jews, he was troubled. And all the people in

Jerusalem were worried too. ⁴Herod called a meeting of all the leading priests and teachers of the law. He asked them where the Christ would be born. ⁵They answered, "In the town of Bethlehem in Judea. The prophet wrote about this in the Scriptures:

⁶"But you, Bethlehem, in the land of Judah,
    you are important among the rulers of Judah.
  A ruler will come from you.
    He will be like a shepherd for my people, the
      Israelites.'"

⁷Then Herod had a secret meeting with the wise men from the east. He learned from them the exact time they first saw the star. ⁸Then Herod sent the wise men to Bethlehem. He said to them, "Go and look carefully to find the child. When you find him, come tell me. Then I can go worship him too."

⁹The wise men heard the king and then left. They saw the same star they had seen in the east. It went before them until it stopped above the place where the child was. ¹⁰When the wise men saw the star, they were filled with joy. ¹¹They went to the house where the child was and saw him with his mother, Mary. They bowed down and worshiped the child. They opened the gifts they brought for him. They gave him treasures of gold, frankincense, and myrrh. ¹²But God warned the wise men in a dream not to go back to Herod. So they went home to their own country by a different way.

The Angel of the Lord
Protects Young Jesus

(From Matthew 2)

2:¹³After they [the wise men] left, an angel of the Lord came to Joseph in a dream. The angel said, "Get up! Take the child and his mother and escape to Egypt. Herod will start looking for the child to kill him. Stay in Egypt until I tell you to return."

¹⁴So Joseph got up and left for Egypt during the night with the child and his mother. ¹⁵Joseph stayed in Egypt until Herod died. This was to make clear the full meaning of what the Lord had said through the prophet. The Lord said, "I called my son out of Egypt."

¹⁶When Herod saw that the wise men had tricked him, he was very angry. So he gave an order to kill all the baby boys in Bethlehem and in all the area around Bethlehem. He said to kill all the boys who were two years old or younger. This was in keeping with the time he learned from the wise men.

¹⁹After Herod died, an angel of the Lord came to Joseph in a dream. This happened while Joseph

was in Egypt. ²⁰The angel said, "Get up! Take the child and his mother and go to Israel. The people who were trying to kill the child are now dead."

²¹So Joseph took the child and his mother and went to Israel. ²²But he heard that Archelaus was now king in Judea. Archelaus became king when his father Herod died. So Joseph was afraid to go there. After being warned in a dream, he went to the area of Galilee. ²³He went to a town called Nazareth and lived there. And so what God had said through the prophets came true: "He will be called a Nazarene."

Jesus in the Wilderness and Then on to Galilee
(From Matthew 4)

4:¹Then the Spirit led Jesus into the desert to be tempted by the devil. ²Jesus ate nothing for 40 days and nights. After this, he was very hungry. ³The devil came to Jesus to tempt him. The devil said, "If you are the Son of God, tell these rocks to become bread."

⁴Jesus answered, "It is written in the Scriptures, 'A person does not live only by eating bread. But a person lives by everything the Lord says.'"

⁵Then the devil led Jesus to the holy city of Jerusalem. He put Jesus on a very high place of the Temple. ⁶The devil said, "If you are the Son of God, jump off. It is written in the Scriptures,

'He has put his angels in charge of you.
  They will catch you with their hands.
And you will not hit your foot on a rock.'"
⁷Jesus answered him, "It also says in the Scriptures, 'Do not test the Lord your God.'"

⁸Then the devil led Jesus to the top of a very high mountain. He showed Jesus all the kingdoms of the world and all the great things that are in those kingdoms. ⁹The devil said, "If you will bow down and worship me, I will give you all these things."

¹⁰Jesus said to the devil, "Go away from me, Satan! It is written in the Scriptures, 'You must worship the Lord your God. Serve only him!'"

¹¹So the devil left Jesus. And then some angels came to Jesus and helped him.

¹²Jesus heard that John had been put in prison. So Jesus went back to Galilee. ¹³ᵃHe left Nazareth and went and lived in Capernaum, a town near Lake Galilee.

¹⁷From that time Jesus began to preach, saying, "Change your hearts and lives, because the kingdom of heaven is coming soon."

¹⁸Jesus was walking by Lake Galilee. He saw two brothers, Simon (called Peter) and Simon's brother Andrew. The brothers were fishermen, and they were fishing in the lake with a net. ¹⁹Jesus said, "Come follow me. I will make you fishermen for men." ²⁰At once Simon and Andrew left their nets and followed him.

²¹Jesus continued walking by Lake Galilee. He saw two other brothers, James and John, the sons of Zebedee. They were in a boat with their father Zebedee, preparing their nets to catch fish. Jesus told them to come with him. ²²At once they left the boat and their father, and they followed Jesus.

²³Jesus went everywhere in Galilee. He taught in the synagogues and preached the Good News about the kingdom of heaven. And he healed all the people's diseases and sicknesses.

The Sermon on the Mount

(From Matthew 5)

5:¹Jesus saw the crowds who were there. He went up on a hill and sat down. His followers came to him. ²Jesus taught the people and said:

³"Those people who know they have great
spiritual needs are happy.
The kingdom of heaven
belongs to them.
⁴Those who are sad now
are happy.
God will comfort them.
⁵Those who are humble are
happy.
The earth will belong to them.
⁶Those who want to do right more than anything
else are happy.
God will fully satisfy them.

[7]Those who give mercy to others are happy.
Mercy will be given to them.
[8]Those who are pure in their thinking are happy.
They will be with God.
[9]Those who work to bring peace are happy.
God will call them his sons.
[10]Those who are treated badly for doing good are happy.
The kingdom of heaven belongs to them.

[11]"People will say bad things about you and hurt you. They will lie and say all kinds of evil things about you because you follow me. But when they do these things to you, you are happy. [12]Rejoice and be glad. You have a great reward waiting for you in heaven. People did the same evil things to the prophets who lived before you.

[13]"You are the salt of the earth. But if the salt loses its salty taste, it cannot be made salty again. It is good for nothing. It must be thrown out for people to walk on.

[14]"You are the light that gives light to the world. A city that is built on a hill cannot be hidden. [15]And people don't hide a light under a bowl. They put the light on a lampstand. Then the light shines for all the people in the house. [16]In the same way, you should be a light for other people. Live so that they will see the good things you do. Live so that they will praise your Father in heaven.

[38]"You have heard that it was said, 'An eye for an eye, and a tooth for a tooth.' [39]But I tell you, don't stand up against an evil person. If someone slaps you on the right cheek, then turn and let him slap the other cheek too. [40]If someone wants to sue you

in court and take your shirt, then let him have your coat too. ⁴¹If a soldier forces you to go with him one mile, then go with him two miles. ⁴²If a person asks you for something, then give it to him. Don't refuse to give to a person who wants to borrow from you.

⁴³"You have heard that it was said, 'Love your neighbor and hate your enemies.' ⁴⁴But I tell you, love your enemies. Pray for those who hurt you. ⁴⁵ᵃIf you do this, then you will be true sons of your Father in heaven."

Jesus Teaches the People
(From Matthew 6 and 7)

6:¹"Be careful! When you do good things, don't do them in front of people to be seen by them. If you do that, then you will have no reward from your Father in heaven.

²"When you give to the poor, don't be like the hypocrites. They blow trumpets before they give so that people will see them. . . . They want other people to honor them. I tell you the truth. Those hypocrites already have their full reward. ³So when you give to the poor, give very secretly. Don't let anyone know what you are doing. ⁴Your giving should be done in secret. Your Father can see what is done in secret, and he will reward you.

⁵"When you pray, don't be like the hypocrites. . . . They want people to see them pray. I tell you the truth. They already have their full reward. ⁶When

you pray, you should go into your room and close the door. Then pray to your Father who cannot be seen. Your Father can see what is done in secret, and he will reward you.

[7]"And when you pray, don't be like those people who don't know God. They continue saying things that mean nothing. They think that God will hear them because of the many things they say. [8]Don't be like them. Your Father knows the things you need before you ask him. [9]So when you pray, you should pray like this:

'Our Father in heaven,
we pray that your name will always be kept
     holy.
[10]We pray that your kingdom will come.
We pray that what you want will be done,
     here on earth as it is in heaven.
[11]Give us the food we need for each day.
[12]Forgive the sins we have done,
     just as we have forgiven those who did wrong to
     us.
[13]Do not cause us to be tested;
  but save us from the Evil One.'
[14]Yes, if you forgive others for the things they do

wrong, then your Father in heaven will also forgive you for the things you do wrong.

[19]"Don't store treasures for yourselves here on earth. Moths and rust will destroy treasures here on earth. And thieves can

break into your house and steal the things you have. ²⁰So store your treasure in heaven. The treasures in heaven cannot be destroyed by moths or rust. And thieves cannot break in and steal that treasure. ²¹Your heart will be where your treasure is.

²⁵"So I tell you, don't worry about the food you need to live. And don't worry about the clothes you need for your body.

³³"The thing you should want most is God's kingdom and doing what God wants. Then all these other things you need will be given to you.

7:¹²"Do for other people the same things you want them to do for you. This is the meaning of the law of Moses and the teaching of the prophets."

Jesus Chooses Matthew and Heals More People

(From Matthew 9)

9:⁹When Jesus was leaving, he saw a man named Matthew. Matthew was sitting in the tax office. Jesus said to him, "Follow me." And Matthew stood up and followed Jesus.

¹⁰Jesus had dinner at Matthew's house. Many tax collectors and "sinners" came and ate with Jesus and his followers. ¹¹The Pharisees saw this and asked Jesus' followers, "Why does your teacher eat with tax collectors and 'sinners'?"

¹²Jesus heard the Pharisees ask this. So he said, "Healthy people don't need a doctor. Only the sick need a doctor. ¹³Go and learn what this means: 'I

want faithful love more than I want animal sacrifices.' I did not come to invite good people. I came to invite sinners."

¹⁸While Jesus was saying these things, a ruler of the synagogue came to him. The ruler bowed down before Jesus and said, "My daughter has just died. But come and touch her with your hand, and she will live again."

¹⁹So Jesus stood up and went with the ruler. Jesus' followers went too.

²⁰Then a woman who had been bleeding for 12 years came behind Jesus and touched the edge of his coat. ²¹She was thinking, "If I can touch his coat, then I will be healed."

²²Jesus turned and saw the woman. He said, "Be happy, dear woman. You are made well because you believed." And the woman was healed at once.

²³Jesus continued along with the ruler and went into the ruler's house. Jesus saw people there who play music for funerals. And he saw many people there crying. ²⁴Jesus said, "Go away. The girl is not dead. She is only asleep." But the people laughed at Jesus. ²⁵After the crowd had been put outside, Jesus went into the girl's room. He took her hand, and she stood up. ²⁶The news about this spread all around the area.

²⁷When Jesus was leaving there, two blind men followed him. They cried out, "Show kindness to us, Son of David!"

²⁸Jesus went inside, and the blind men went with him. He asked the men, "Do you believe that I can make you see again?"

They answered, "Yes, Lord."

[29]Then Jesus touched their eyes and said, "You believe that I can make you see again. So this will happen." [30]Then the men were able to see. But Jesus warned them very strongly, saying, "Don't tell anyone about this." [31]But the blind men left and spread the news about Jesus all around that area.

[35]Jesus traveled through all the towns and villages. He taught in their synagogues and told people the Good News about the kingdom. And he healed all kinds of diseases and sicknesses. [36]He saw the crowds of people and felt sorry for them because they were worried and helpless. They were like sheep without a shepherd. [37]Jesus said to his followers, "There are many people to harvest, but there are only a few workers to help harvest them. [38]God owns the harvest. Pray to him that he will send more workers to help gather his harvest."

Jesus Tells Stories

(From Matthew 13)

13:[3b][Jesus] said: "A farmer went out to plant his seed. [4]While he was planting, some seed fell by the road. The birds came and ate all that seed. [5]Some seed fell on rocky ground, where there wasn't enough dirt. That seed grew very fast, because the ground was not deep. ⁶But when the sun rose, the plants dried up because they did not have deep roots. ⁷Some other seed fell among thorny weeds. The weeds grew and choked the good plants. ⁸ᵃSome other seed fell on good ground where it grew and became grain.

¹⁹"What is the seed that fell by the road? That seed is like the person who hears the teaching about the kingdom but does not understand it. The Evil One comes and takes away the things that were planted in that person's heart. ²⁰And what is the seed that fell on rocky ground? That seed is like the person who hears the teaching and quickly accepts it with joy. ²¹But he does not let the teaching go deep into his life. . . . When trouble or persecution comes because of the teaching he accepted, then he quickly gives up. ²²ᵃAnd what is the seed that fell among the thorny weeds? That seed is like the person who hears the teaching but lets worries about this life and love of money stop that teaching from growing. ²³ᵃBut what is the seed that fell on the good ground? That seed is like the person who hears the teaching and understands it. That person grows and produces fruit."

²⁴Then Jesus told them another story. He said, "The kingdom of heaven is like a man who planted good seed in his field. ²⁵That night, when everyone was asleep, his enemy came and planted weeds among

the wheat. Then the enemy went away. ²⁶Later, the wheat grew and heads of grain grew on the wheat plants. But at the same time the weeds also grew. ²⁸ᵇThe servants asked, 'Do you want us to pull up the weeds?' ²⁹The man answered, 'No, because when you pull up the weeds, you might also pull up the wheat. ³⁰Let the weeds and the wheat grow together until the harvest time. At harvest time . . . gather the weeds and tie them together to be burned. Then gather the wheat and bring it to my barn.'"

³⁷Jesus [said to his disciples], "The man who planted the good seed in the field is the Son of Man. ³⁸The field is the world. And the good seed are all of God's children. . . . The weeds are those people who belong to the Evil One. ³⁹And the enemy who planted the bad seed is the devil. The harvest time is the end of the world. And the workers who gather are God's angels.

⁴⁰ᵇ"It will be this way at the end of the world. ⁴¹The Son of Man will send out his angels. They will gather out of his kingdom all who cause sin and all who do evil. ⁴³Then the good people will shine like the sun in the kingdom of their Father. You people who hear me, listen!"

Jesus Feeds More Than 5,000 People and Walks on Water
(From Matthew 14)

14:¹³ᵇJesus left in a boat. He went to a lonely place by himself. But when the crowds heard about it, they followed him on foot from the towns.

[14]When Jesus arrived, he saw a large crowd. He felt sorry for them and healed those who were sick.

[15]Late that afternoon, his followers came to Jesus and said, "No one lives in this place. And it is already late. Send the people away so they can go to the towns and buy food for themselves."

[16]Jesus answered, "They don't need to go away. You give them some food to eat."

[17]The followers answered, "But we have only five loaves of bread and two fish."

[18]Jesus said, "Bring the bread and the fish to me." [19]Then he told the people to sit down on the grass. He took the five loaves of bread and the two fish. Then he looked to heaven and thanked God for the food. Jesus divided the loaves of bread. He gave them to his followers, and they gave the bread to the people. [20]All the people ate and were satisfied. After they finished eating, the followers filled 12 baskets with the pieces of food that were not eaten.

²¹There were about 5,000 men there who ate, as well as women and children.

²²Then Jesus made his followers get into the boat. He told them to go ahead of him to the other side of the lake. Jesus stayed there to tell the people they could go home. ²³After he said good-bye to them, he went alone up into the hills to pray. It was late, and Jesus was there alone. ²⁴By this time, the boat was already far away on the lake. The boat was having trouble because of the waves, and the wind was blowing against it.

²⁵Between three and six o'clock in the morning, Jesus' followers were still in the boat. Jesus came to them. He was walking on the water. ²⁶When the followers saw him walking on the water, they were afraid. They said, "It's a ghost!" and cried out in fear.

²⁷But Jesus quickly spoke to them. He said, "Have courage! It is I! Don't be afraid."

²⁸Peter said, "Lord, if that is really you, then tell me to come to you on the water."

²⁹Jesus said, "Come."

And Peter left the boat and walked on the water to Jesus. ³⁰But when Peter saw the wind and the waves, he became afraid and began to sink. He shouted, "Lord, save me!"

³¹Then Jesus reached out his hand and caught Peter. Jesus said, "Your faith is small. Why did you doubt?"

³²After Peter and Jesus were in the boat, the wind became calm. ³³Then those who were in the boat worshiped Jesus and said, "Truly you are the Son of God!"

Jesus Is the Promised One

(From Matthew 16 and 17)

16:¹³Jesus went to the area of Caesarea Philippi. He said to his followers, "I am the Son of Man. Who do the people say I am?"

¹⁴They answered, "Some people say you are John the Baptist. Others say you are Elijah. And others say that you are Jeremiah or one of the prophets."

¹⁵Then Jesus asked them, "And who do you say I am?"

¹⁶Simon Peter answered, "You are the Christ, the Son of the living God."

¹⁷Jesus answered, "You are blessed, Simon son of Jonah. No person taught you that. My Father in heaven showed you who I am. ¹⁸So I tell you, you are Peter. And I will build my church on this rock. The power of death will not be able to defeat my church. ¹⁹I will give you the keys of the kingdom of heaven. The things you don't allow on earth will be the things that God does not allow. The things you allow on earth will be the things that God allows."

²⁰Then Jesus warned his followers not to tell anyone that he was the Christ.

²¹From that time on Jesus began telling his followers that he must go to Jerusalem. He explained that the older Jewish leaders, the leading priests, and the teachers of the law would make him suffer many things. And he told them that he must be killed. Then, on the third day, he would be raised from death.

²⁴Then Jesus said to his followers, "If anyone wants to follow me, he must say 'no' to the things

he wants. He must be willing even to die on a cross, and he must follow me."

17:¹Six days later, Jesus took Peter, James, and John the brother of James up on a high mountain. They were all alone there. ²While they watched, Jesus was changed. His face became bright like the sun. And his clothes became white as light. ³Then two men were there, talking with him. The men were Moses and Elijah.

⁴Peter said to Jesus, "Lord, it is good that we are here. If you want, I will put three tents here—one for you, one for Moses, and one for Elijah."

⁵While Peter was talking, a bright cloud covered them. A voice came from the cloud. The voice said, "This is my Son and I love him. I am very pleased with him. Obey him!"

⁶The followers with Jesus heard the voice. They were so frightened that they fell to the ground. ⁷But Jesus went to them and touched them. He said, "Stand up. Don't be afraid." ⁸When the followers looked up, they saw Jesus was now alone.

⁹When Jesus and the followers were coming down the mountain, Jesus commanded them, "Don't tell anyone about the things you saw on the mountain. Wait until the Son of Man has been raised from death. Then you may tell."

Jesus Rides into Jerusalem on a Donkey

(From Matthew 21)

21:¹Jesus and his followers were coming closer to Jerusalem. But first they stopped at Bethphage at the hill called the Mount of Olives. From there Jesus sent two of his followers into the town. ²He said to them, "Go to the town you can see there. When you enter it, you will find a donkey tied there with its colt. Untie them and bring them to me. ³If anyone asks you why you are taking the donkeys, tell him, 'The Master needs them. He will send them back soon.'"

⁴This was to make clear the full meaning of what the prophet said:

⁵"Tell the people of Jerusalem,
'Your king is coming to you.
He is gentle and riding on a donkey.
He is on the colt of a donkey.'"

⁶The followers went and did what Jesus told them to do. ⁷They brought the donkey and the colt to Jesus. They laid their coats on the donkeys, and Jesus sat on them. ⁸Many people spread their coats on the road before Jesus. Others cut branches from the trees and spread them on the road. ⁹Some of the people were walking ahead of Jesus. Others were

walking behind him. All the people were shouting,
"Praise to the Son of David!
God bless the One who comes in the name of the
Lord!
Praise to God in heaven!"
[10]Then Jesus went into Jerusalem. The city was
filled with excitement. The people asked, "Who is
this man?"
[11]The crowd answered, "This man is Jesus. He is
the prophet from the town of Nazareth in Galilee."

The Plan to Kill Jesus
(From Matthew 26)

26:[1b][Jesus] told his followers, [2]"You know that
the day after tomorrow is the day of the Passover
Feast. On that day the Son of Man will be given to
his enemies to be killed on a cross."
[3]Then the leading priests and the older Jewish
leaders had a meeting at the palace of the high
priest. The high priest's name was Caiaphas. [4]At
the meeting, they planned to set a trap to arrest
Jesus and kill him. [5]But they said, "We must not do
it during the feast. The people might cause a riot."
[14]Then 1 of the 12 followers went to talk to the
leading priests. This was the follower named
Judas Iscariot. [15]He said, "I will give Jesus to you.
What will you pay me for doing this?" The priests
gave Judas 30 silver coins. [16]After that, Judas
waited for the best time to give Jesus to the
priests.
[20]In the evening Jesus was sitting at the table

with his 12 followers. ²¹They were all eating. Then Jesus said, "I tell you the truth. One of you 12 will turn against me."

²²This made the followers very sad. Each one said to Jesus, "Surely, Lord, I am not the one who will turn against you. Am I?"

²³Jesus answered, "The man who has dipped his hand with me into the bowl is the one who will turn against me. ²⁴The Son of Man will die. The Scriptures say this will happen. But how terrible it will be for the person who gives the Son of Man to be killed. It would be better for him if he had never been born."

²⁵Then Judas said to Jesus, "Teacher, surely I am not the one. Am I?" (Judas is the one who would give Jesus to his enemies.)

Jesus answered, "Yes, it is you."

⁴⁷ᵇJudas came up [to Jesus]. . . . [Judas] had many people with him. They had been sent from the leading priests and the older leaders of the people. They carried swords and clubs. ⁴⁸Judas had planned to give them a signal. He had said, "The man I kiss is Jesus. Arrest him." ⁴⁹At once Judas went to Jesus and said, "Greetings, Teacher!" Then Judas kissed him.

⁵⁰Jesus answered, "Friend, do the thing you came to do."

Then the men came and grabbed Jesus and arrested him. ⁵¹When that happened, one of Jesus' followers reached for his sword and pulled it out. The follower struck the servant of the high priest with the sword and cut off his ear.

[52]Jesus said to the man, "Put your sword back in its place. All who use swords will be killed with swords. [53]Surely you know that I could ask my Father, and he would give me more than 12 armies of angels. [54]But this thing must happen in this way so that it will be as the Scriptures say."

[56b]Then all of Jesus' followers left him and ran away.

Peter Denies Jesus

(From Matthew 26)

26:[57]Those men who arrested Jesus led him to the house of Caiaphas, the high priest. The teachers of the law and the older Jewish leaders were gathered there. [58]Peter followed Jesus but did not go near him. He followed Jesus to the courtyard of the high priest's house. He sat down with the guards to see what would happen to Jesus.

[59]The leading priests and the Jewish council tried to find something false against Jesus so that they could kill him. [60]Many people came and told lies about him. But the council could find no real reason to kill Jesus. Then two people came and said, [61]"This man said, 'I can destroy the Temple of God and build it again in three days.'"

[62]Then the high priest stood up and said to Jesus, "Aren't you going to answer? Don't you have some-

thing to say about their charges against you?" [63]But Jesus said nothing.

Again the high priest said to Jesus, "You must swear to this. I command you by the power of the living God to tell us the truth. Tell us, are you the Christ, the Son of God?"

[64]Jesus answered, "Yes, I am. But I tell you, in the future you will see the Son of Man sitting at the right hand of God, the Powerful One. And you will see him coming in clouds in the sky."

[65a]When the high priest heard this, he was very angry. He tore his clothes and said, "This man has said things that are against God! We don't need any more witnesses. You all heard him say these things against God. [66]What do you think?"

The people answered, "He is guilty, and he must die."

[67]Then the people there spit in Jesus' face and beat him with their fists. Others slapped Jesus.

[69]At that time, Peter was sitting in the courtyard. A servant girl came to him and said, "You were with Jesus, that man from Galilee."

[70]But Peter said that he was never with Jesus. He said this to all the people there. Peter said, "I don't know what you are talking about."

[71]Then he left the courtyard. At the gate, another girl saw him. She said to the people there, "This man was with Jesus of Nazareth."

[72]Again, Peter said that he was never with Jesus. Peter said, "I swear that I don't know this man Jesus!"

[73]A short time later, some people standing there went to Peter. They said, "We know you are one of

those men who followed Jesus. We know this because of the way you talk."

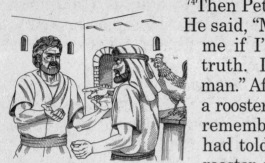

⁷⁴Then Peter began to curse. He said, "May a curse fall on me if I'm not telling the truth. I don't know the man." After Peter said this, a rooster crowed. ⁷⁵Then he remembered what Jesus had told him: "Before the rooster crows, you will say three times that you don't know me." Then Peter went outside and cried painfully.

Jesus Is Tried and Crucified

(From Matthew 27)

27:¹Early the next morning, all the leading priests and older leaders of the people decided to kill Jesus. ²They tied him, led him away, and turned him over to Pilate, the governor.

¹¹Jesus stood before Pilate. . . . Pilate asked him, "Are you the King of the Jews?"

Jesus answered, "Yes, I am."

¹²When the leading priests and the older leaders accused Jesus, he said nothing.

¹³So Pilate said to Jesus, "Don't you hear these people accusing you of all these things?"

¹⁴But Jesus said nothing in answer to Pilate. Pilate was very surprised at this.

¹⁵Every year at the time of Passover the governor

would free one person from prison. This was always a person the people wanted to be set free. [16]At that time there was a man in prison who was known to be very bad. His name was Barabbas. [17b]Pilate said, "Which man do you want to free: Barabbas, or Jesus who is called the Christ?"

[20]But the leading priests and older leaders told the crowd to ask for Barabbas to be freed and for Jesus to be killed.

[21]Pilate said, "I have Barabbas and Jesus. Which do you want me to set free for you?"

The people answered, "Barabbas!"

[22]Pilate asked, "What should I do with Jesus, the one called the Christ?"

They all answered, "Kill him on a cross!"

[24]Pilate saw that he could do nothing about this, and a riot was starting. So he took some water and washed his hands in front of the crowd. Then he said, "I am not guilty of this man's death. You are the ones who are causing it!"

[26]Then Pilate freed Barabbas. Pilate told some of the soldiers to beat Jesus with whips. Then he gave Jesus to the soldiers to be killed on a cross.

[32]The soldiers were going out of the city with Jesus. They forced another man to carry the cross to be used for Jesus. This man was Simon, from Cyrene. [33]They all came to the place called Golgotha. (Golgotha means the Place of the Skull.) [35]The soldiers nailed Jesus to a cross. They

threw lots to decide who would get his clothes. [36]The soldiers sat there and continued watching him. [37]They put a sign above Jesus' head with the charge against him written on it. The sign read: "THIS IS JESUS, THE KING OF THE JEWS."

[45]At noon the whole country became dark. This darkness lasted for three hours. [46]About three o'clock Jesus cried out in a loud voice, " . . . My God, my God, why have you left me alone?"

[50]Again Jesus cried out in a loud voice. Then he died.

[51]Then the curtain in the Temple split into two pieces. . . . Also, the earth shook and rocks broke apart.

[54]The army officer and the soldiers guarding Jesus saw this earthquake and everything else that happened. They were very frightened and said, "He really was the Son of God!"

Jesus Rises from the Tomb
(From Matthew 27 and 28)

27:[57]That evening a rich man named Joseph came to Jerusalem. He was a follower of Jesus from the town of Arimathea. [58]Joseph went to Pilate and asked to have Jesus' body. Pilate gave orders for the soldiers to give it to Joseph. [59]Then Joseph took the body and wrapped it in a clean linen cloth. [60]He put Jesus' body in a new tomb that he had cut in a wall of rock. He rolled a very large stone to block the entrance of the tomb. Then

Joseph went away. ⁶¹Mary Magdalene and the other woman named Mary were sitting near the tomb.

⁶²That day was the day called Preparation Day. The next day, the leading priests and the Pharisees went to Pilate. ⁶³They said, "Sir, we remember that while that liar was still alive he said, 'After three days I will rise from death.' ⁶⁴So give the order for the tomb to be guarded closely till the third day. His followers might come and steal the body. Then they could tell the people that he has risen from death. That lie would be even worse than the first one."

⁶⁵Pilate said, "Take some soldiers and go guard the tomb the best way you know." ⁶⁶So they all went to the tomb and made it safe from thieves. They did this by sealing the stone in the entrance and then putting soldiers there to guard it.

28:¹The day after the Sabbath day was the first day of the week. At dawn on the first day, Mary Magdalene and another woman named Mary went to look at the tomb.

²At that time there was a strong earthquake. An angel of the Lord came down

from heaven. The angel went to the tomb and rolled the stone away from the entrance. Then he sat on the stone. ³He was shining as bright as lightning. His clothes were white as snow. ⁴The soldiers guarding the tomb were very frightened of the angel. They shook with fear and then became like dead men.

⁵The angel said to the women, "Don't be afraid. I know that you are looking for Jesus, the one who was killed on the cross. ⁶But he is not here. He has risen from death as he said he would. Come and see the place where his body was. ⁷And go quickly and tell his followers. Say to them: 'Jesus has risen from death. He is going into Galilee. He will be there before you. You will see him there.'" Then the angel said, "Now I have told you."

⁸The women left the tomb quickly. They were afraid, but they were also very happy. They ran to tell Jesus' followers what had happened. ⁹Suddenly, Jesus met them and said, "Greetings." The women came up to Jesus, took hold of his feet, and worshiped him. ¹⁰Then Jesus said to them, "Don't be afraid. Go and tell my brothers to go on to Galilee. They will see me there."

Jesus Heals the Sick

(From Mark 1 and 2)

1:²¹Jesus and his followers went to Capernaum. On the Sabbath day Jesus went to the synagogue and began to teach. ²²The people there were amazed at his teaching. He did not teach like their teachers of the law. He taught like a person who had authority. ²³While he was in the synagogue, a man was there who had an evil spirit in him. The man shouted, ²⁴"Jesus of Nazareth! What do you want with us? Did you come to destroy us? I know who you are—God's Holy One!"

²⁵Jesus said strongly, "Be quiet! Come out of the man!" ²⁶The evil spirit made the man shake violently. Then the spirit gave a loud cry and came out of him.

²⁷The people were amazed. They asked each other, "What is happening here? This man is teaching something new. And he teaches with authority. He even gives commands to evil spirits, and they obey him." ²⁸And the news about Jesus spread quickly everywhere in the area of Galilee.

²⁹Jesus and his followers left the synagogue. They all went at once with James and John to the home of Simon and Andrew. ³⁰Simon's mother-in-law was sick in bed with a fever. The people there told Jesus about her. ³¹So Jesus went to her bed, took her hand, and helped her up. Immediately the fever left her, and she was healed. Then she began serving them.

2:¹A few days later, Jesus came back to Capernaum. The news spread that he was home. ²So many people gathered to hear him preach that the house was full. There was no place to stand, not even outside the door. Jesus was teaching them. ³Some people came, bringing a paralyzed man to Jesus. Four of them were carrying the paralyzed man. ⁴But they could not get to Jesus because of the crowd. So they went to the roof above Jesus and made a hole in the roof. Then they lowered the mat with the paralyzed man on it. [5]Jesus saw that these men had great faith. So he said to the paralyzed man, "Young man, your sins are forgiven."

[6]Some of the teachers of the law were sitting there. They saw what Jesus did, and they said to themselves, [7]"Why does this man say things like that? He is saying things that are against God. Only God can forgive sins."

[8]At once Jesus knew what these teachers of the law were thinking. So he said to them, "Why are you thinking these things? [9]Which is easier: to tell this paralyzed man, 'Your sins are forgiven,' or to tell him, 'Stand up. Take your mat and walk'? [10]But I will prove to you that the Son of Man has authority on earth to forgive sins." So Jesus said to the paralyzed man, [11]"I tell you, stand up. Take your mat and go home." [12a]Immediately the paralyzed man stood up. He took his mat and walked out while everyone was watching him.

Healing and Teaching on the Sabbath

(From Mark 2—4)

2:[23]On the Sabbath day, Jesus was walking through some grainfields. His followers were with him and picked some grain to eat. 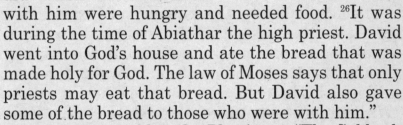 ²⁴The Pharisees saw this and said to Jesus, "Why are your followers doing what is not lawful on the Sabbath?"

²⁵Jesus answered, "You have read what David did when he and those with him were hungry and needed food. ²⁶It was during the time of Abiathar the high priest. David went into God's house and ate the bread that was made holy for God. The law of Moses says that only priests may eat that bread. But David also gave some of the bread to those who were with him."

²⁷Then Jesus said to the Pharisees, "The Sabbath day was made to help people. They were not made to be ruled by the Sabbath day. ²⁸The Son of Man is Lord even of the Sabbath."

3:¹Another time when Jesus went into a synagogue, a man with a crippled hand was there. ²Some people there wanted to see Jesus do something wrong so they could accuse him. They watched him closely to see if he would heal the man on the Sabbath day.

³Jesus said to the man with the crippled hand, "Stand up here in front of everyone."

⁴Then Jesus asked the people, "Which is right on the Sabbath day: to do good, or to do evil? Is it right to save a life or to destroy one?" But they said nothing to answer him.

⁵Jesus was angry as he looked at the people. But

he felt very sad because they were stubborn. Then he said to the man, "Let me see your hand." The man put his hand out for Jesus, and it was healed. ⁶Then the Pharisees left and began making plans with the Herodians about a way to kill Jesus.

4:¹Another time Jesus began teaching by the lake. A great crowd gathered around him. So he got into a boat and went out on the lake. All the people stayed on the shore close to the water. ²Jesus used many stories to teach them.

²⁶Then Jesus said, "The kingdom of God is like a man who plants seed in the ground. ²⁷The seed comes up and grows night and day. It doesn't matter whether the man is asleep or awake; the seed still grows. The man does not know how it grows. ²⁸Without any help, the earth produces grain. First the plant grows, then the head, and then all the grain in the head. ²⁹When the grain is ready, the man cuts it. This is the harvest time."

³⁰Then Jesus said, "How can I show you what the kingdom of God is like? What story can I use to explain it? ³¹The kingdom of God is like a mustard seed. The mustard seed is the smallest seed you plant in the ground. ³²But when you plant this seed, it grows and becomes the largest of all garden plants. It produces large branches. Even the wild birds can make nests in it and be protected from the sun."

³³Jesus used many stories like these to teach them. He taught them all that they could understand. ³⁴He always used stories to teach them. But when he and his followers were alone together, Jesus explained everything to them.

A Storm and Evil Spirits Are No Match for Jesus

(From Mark 4 and 5)

4:³⁵That evening, Jesus said to his followers, "Come with me across the lake." ^{36a}He and the followers left the people there. They went in the boat that Jesus was already sitting in. ³⁷A very strong wind came up on the lake. The waves began coming over the sides and into the boat. It was almost full of water. ³⁸Jesus was at the back of the boat, sleeping with his head on a pillow. The followers went to him and woke him. They said, "Teacher, do you care about us? We will drown!"

³⁹Jesus stood up and commanded the wind and the waves to stop. He said, "Quiet! Be still!" Then the wind stopped, and the lake became calm.

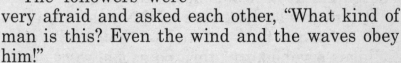

⁴⁰Jesus said to his followers, "Why are you afraid? Do you still have no faith?" ⁴¹The followers were very afraid and asked each other, "What kind of man is this? Even the wind and the waves obey him!"

5:¹Jesus and his followers went across the lake to the region of the Gerasene people. ²When Jesus got out of the boat, a man came to him from the caves where dead people were buried. This man, who lived in the caves, had an evil spirit living in him. ³No one could tie him up, not even with a chain. ⁴Many times people had used chains to tie the man's hands and feet. But he always broke the chains off. No one was strong enough to control him. ⁵Day and night he would wander around the burial caves and on the hills, screaming and cutting himself with stones. ⁶While Jesus was still far away, the man saw him. He ran to Jesus and knelt down before him. ⁷⁻⁸Jesus said to the man, "You evil spirit, come out of that man."

But the man shouted in a loud voice, "What do you want with me, Jesus, Son of the Most High God? I beg you, promise God that you will not punish me!"

⁹Then Jesus asked the man, "What is your name?"

The man answered, "My name is Legion, because I have many spirits in me."

¹¹A large herd of pigs was eating on a hill near there. ¹²The evil spirits begged Jesus, "Send us to the pigs. Let us go into them." ¹³So Jesus allowed them to do this. The evil spirits left the man and went into the pigs. Then the herd of pigs rushed down the hill into the lake and were drowned. There were about 2,000 pigs in that herd.

¹⁴The men who took care of the pigs ran away. They went to the town and to the countryside, telling everyone about this. So people went out to see what had happened. ¹⁵They came to Jesus and saw the man who had had the many evil spirits. The man was sitting there, clothed and in his right mind. The people were frightened. ¹⁶Some people

were there who saw what Jesus had done. They told the others what had happened to the man who had the demons living in him. And they also told about the pigs.

Jesus Teaches About Entering the Kingdom of God

(From Mark 10)

10:¹³Some people brought their small children to Jesus so he could touch them. But his followers told the people to stop bringing their children to him. ¹⁴When Jesus saw this, he was displeased. He said to them, "Let the little children come to me. Don't stop them. The kingdom of God belongs to people who are like these little children.  ¹⁵I tell you the truth. You must accept the kingdom of God as a little child accepts things, or you will never enter it." ¹⁶Then Jesus took the children in his arms. He put his hands on them and blessed them.

¹⁷Jesus started to leave, but a man ran to him and fell on his knees before Jesus. The man asked, "Good teacher, what must I do to get the life that never ends?"

¹⁸Jesus answered, "Why do you call me good? No one is good except God alone. ¹⁹You know the commands: 'You must not murder anyone. You must

not be guilty of adultery. You must not steal. You must not tell lies about your neighbor in court. You must not cheat. Honor your father and mother.'"

²⁰The man said, "Teacher, I have obeyed all these commands since I was a boy."

²¹Jesus looked straight at the man and loved him. Jesus said, "There is still one more thing you need to do. Go and sell everything you have, and give the money to the poor. You will have a reward in heaven. Then come and follow me."

²²He was very sad to hear Jesus say this, and he left. The man was sad because he was very rich.

²³Then Jesus looked at his followers and said, "How hard it will be for those who are rich to enter the kingdom of God!"

²⁴The followers were amazed at what Jesus said. But he said again, "My children, it is very hard to enter the kingdom of God! ²⁵And it will be very hard for a rich person to enter the kingdom of God. It would be easier for a camel to go through the eye of a needle!"

²⁶The followers were even more amazed and said to each other, "Then who can be saved?"

²⁷Jesus looked straight at them and said, "This is something that men cannot do. But God can do it. God can do all things."

A Woman Pours Oil on Jesus' Head
(From Mark 14)

14:³ Jesus was in Bethany. He was at dinner in the house of Simon, who had a harmful skin disease. While Jesus was there, a woman came to him. She had an alabaster jar filled with very expensive perfume, made of pure nard. The woman opened the jar and poured the perfume on Jesus' head.

⁴Some of those who were there saw this and became angry. They complained to each other, saying, "Why waste that perfume? ⁵It was worth a full year's work. It could be sold, and the money could be given to the poor." They spoke to the woman sharply.

⁶Jesus said, "Don't bother the woman. Why are you troubling her? She did a beautiful thing for me. ⁷You will always have the poor with you. You can help them anytime you want. But you will not always have me. ⁸This woman did the only thing she could do for me. She poured perfume on my body. She did this before I die to prepare me for burial. ⁹I tell you the truth. The Good News will be told to people in all the world. And in every place it is preached, what this woman has done will be told. And people will remember her."

The Last Supper

(From Mark 14)

14:¹² It was now the first day of the Feast of Unleavened Bread. This was a time when the Jews

217

always sacrificed the Passover lambs. Jesus' followers came to him. They said, "We will go and prepare everything for the Passover Feast. Where do you want to eat the feast?"

[13]Jesus sent two of his followers and said to them, "Go into the city. A man carrying a jar of water will meet you. Follow him. [14]He will go into a house. Tell the owner of the house, 'The Teacher asks that you show us the room where he and his followers can eat the Passover Feast.' [15]The owner will show you a large room upstairs. This room is ready. Prepare the food for us there."

[16]So the followers left and went into the city. Everything happened as Jesus had said. So they prepared the Passover Feast.

[17]In the evening, Jesus went to that house with the 12.

[22]While they were eating, Jesus took some bread. He thanked God for it and broke it. Then he gave it to his followers and said, "Take it. This bread is my body."

[23]Then Jesus took a cup. He thanked God for it and gave it to the followers. All the followers drank from the cup.

[24]Then Jesus said, "This is my blood which begins the new agreement that God makes with his people. This blood is poured out for many. [25]I tell you the truth. I will not drink of this fruit of the vine

again until that day when I drink it new in the kingdom of God."

²⁶They sang a hymn and went out to the Mount of Olives.

Jesus' Followers Run Away

(From Mark 14)

14:²⁷Then Jesus told the followers, "You will all lose your faith in me. It is written in the Scriptures:
  'I will kill the shepherd,
    and the sheep will
      scatter.'
²⁸But after I rise from death, I will go ahead of you into Galilee."

²⁹Peter said, "All the other followers may lose their faith. But I will not."

³⁰Jesus answered, "I tell you the truth. Tonight you will say you don't know me. You will say this three times before the rooster crows twice."

³¹But Peter answered strongly, "I will never say that I don't know you! I will even die with you!" And all the other followers said the same thing.

³²Jesus and his followers went to a place called Gethsemane. He said to his followers, "Sit here while I pray." ³³Jesus told Peter, James, and John to come with him. Then Jesus began to be very sad and troubled. ³⁴He said to them, "I am full of sorrow.

My heart is breaking with sadness. Stay here and watch."

[35]Jesus walked a little farther away from them. Then he fell on the ground and prayed. He prayed that, if possible, he would not have this time of suffering. [36]He prayed, "Abba, Father! You can do all things. Let me not have this cup of suffering. But do what you want, not what I want."

[37]Then Jesus went back to his followers. He found them asleep. He said to Peter, "Simon, why are you sleeping? You could not stay awake with me for one hour? [38]Stay awake and pray that you will not be tempted. Your spirit wants to do what is right, but your body is weak."

[39]Again Jesus went away and prayed the same thing. [40]Then he went back to the followers. Again he found them asleep because their eyes were very heavy. And they did not know what to say to Jesus.

[41]After Jesus prayed a third time, he went back to his followers. He said to them, "You are still sleeping and resting? That's enough! The time has come for the Son of Man to be given to sinful people. [42]Get up! We must go. Here comes the man who has turned against me."

[43]While Jesus was still speaking, Judas came up. Judas was 1 of the 12 followers. He had many people with him. They were sent from the leading priests, the teachers of the law, and the older Jewish leaders. Those with Judas had swords and clubs.

[46]Then the men grabbed Jesus and arrested him.

[48]Then Jesus said, "You came to get me with swords and clubs as if I were a criminal. [49]Every

day I was with you teaching in the Temple. You did not arrest me there. But all these things have happened to make the Scriptures come true." ⁵⁰Then all of Jesus' followers left him and ran away.

⁵¹A young man, wearing only a linen cloth, was following Jesus. The people also grabbed him. ⁵²But the cloth he was wearing came off, and he ran away naked.

God Promises a Son
for Zechariah and Elizabeth

(From Luke 1)

1:⁵During the time Herod ruled Judea, there was a priest named Zechariah. . . . Zechariah's wife came from the family of Aaron. Her name was Elizabeth. ⁶Zechariah and Elizabeth truly did what God said was good. They did everything the Lord commanded and told people to do. They were without fault in keeping his law. ⁷But Zechariah and Elizabeth had no children. Elizabeth could not have a baby; and both of them were very old.

⁸Zechariah was serving as a priest before God for his group. It was his group's time to serve. ⁹According to the custom of the priests, he was chosen to go into the Temple of the Lord and burn incense. ¹⁰There were a great many people outside praying at the time the incense was offered. ¹¹Then, on the right side of the incense table, an angel of the Lord came and stood before Zechariah.

[12]When he saw the angel, Zechariah was confused and frightened. [13]But the angel said to him, "Zechariah, don't be afraid. Your prayer has been heard by God. Your wife, Elizabeth, will give birth to a son. You will name him John. [14]You will be very happy. Many people will be happy because of his birth. [15]John will be a  great man for the Lord. He will never drink wine or beer. Even at the time John is born, he will be filled with the Holy Spirit. [16]He will help many people of Israel return to the Lord their God. [17]He himself will go first before the Lord. John will be powerful in spirit like Elijah. He will make peace between fathers and their children. He will bring those who are not obeying God back to the right way of thinking. He will make people ready for the coming of the Lord."

[18]Zechariah said to the angel, "How can I know that what you say is true? I am an old man, and my wife is old, too."

[19]The angel answered him, "I am Gabriel. I stand before God. God sent me to talk to you and to tell you this good news. [20]Now, listen! You will not be able to talk until the day these things happen. You will lose your speech because you did not believe what I told you. But these things will really happen."

[21]Outside, the people were still waiting for Zechariah. They were surprised that he was stay-

ing so long in the Temple. ²²Then Zechariah came outside, but he could not speak to them. So they knew that he had seen a vision in the Temple. Zechariah could not speak. He could only make signs to them. ²³When his time of service as a priest was finished, he went home.

²⁴Later, Zechariah's wife, Elizabeth, became pregnant. She did not go out of her house for five months. Elizabeth said, ²⁵"Look what the Lord has done for me! My people were ashamed of me, but now the Lord has taken away that shame."

An Angel Visits Mary

(From Luke 1)

1:²⁶⁻²⁷During Elizabeth's sixth month of pregnancy, God sent the angel Gabriel to a [young unmarried woman] who lived in Nazareth, a town in Galilee. She was engaged to marry a man named Joseph from the family of David. Her name was Mary. ²⁸The angel came to her and said, "Greetings! The Lord has blessed you and is with you."

²⁹But Mary was very confused by what the angel said. Mary wondered, "What does this mean?"

³⁰The angel said to her, "Don't be afraid, Mary, because God is pleased with you. ³¹Listen! You will become pregnant. You will give birth to a son, and you will name him Jesus. ³²He will be great, and people will call him the Son of the Most High. The Lord God will give him the throne of King David,

his ancestor. ³³He will rule over the people of Jacob forever. His kingdom will never end."

³⁴Mary said to the angel, "How will this happen? I am [not married]!"

³⁵The angel said to Mary, "The Holy Spirit will come upon you, and the power of the Most High will cover you. The baby will be holy. He will be called the Son of God. ³⁶Now listen! Elizabeth, your relative, is very old. But she is also pregnant with a son. Everyone thought she could not have a baby, but she has been pregnant for six months. ³⁷God can do everything!"

³⁸Mary said, "I am the servant girl of the Lord. Let this happen to me as you say!" Then the angel went away.

³⁹Mary got up and went quickly to a town in the mountains of Judea. ⁴⁰She went to Zechariah's house and greeted Elizabeth. ⁴¹When Elizabeth heard Mary's greeting, the unborn baby inside Elizabeth jumped. Then Elizabeth was filled with the Holy Spirit. ⁴²She cried out in a loud voice, "God has blessed you more than any other woman. And God has blessed the baby which you will give birth to. ⁴³You are the mother of my Lord, and you

have come to me! Why has something so good happened to me? [44]When I heard your voice, the baby inside me jumped with joy. [45]You are blessed because you believed what the Lord said to you would really happen."

[46]Then Mary said,

"My soul praises the Lord;
[47] my heart is happy because God is my Savior.
[48]I am not important, but God has shown his care
      for me, his servant girl.

From now on, all people will say that I am blessed,
[49] because the Powerful One has done great things for me.

His name is holy.
[50]God will always give mercy
    to those who worship him.
[54]God has helped his people Israel who serve him.
    He gave them his mercy.
[55]God has done what he promised to our ancestors,
    to Abraham and to his children forever."

[56]Mary stayed with Elizabeth for about three months and then returned home.

Jesus Is Born

(From Luke 2)

2:[1]At that time, Augustus Caesar sent an order to all people in the countries that were under

Roman rule. The order said that they must list their names in a register. ²This was the first registration taken while Quirinius was governor of Syria. ³And everyone went to their own towns to be registered.

⁴So Joseph left Nazareth, a town in Galilee. He went to the town of Bethlehem in Judea. This town was known as the town of David. Joseph went there because he was from the family of David. ⁵Joseph registered with Mary because she was engaged to marry him. (Mary was now pregnant.)

⁶While Joseph and Mary were in Bethlehem, the time came for her to have the baby. ⁷She gave birth to her first son. There were no rooms left in the inn. So she wrapped the baby with cloths and laid him in a box where animals are fed.

⁸That night, some shepherds were in the fields nearby watching their sheep. ⁹An angel of the Lord stood before them. The glory of the Lord was shining around them, and suddenly they became very frightened. ¹⁰The angel said to them, "Don't be afraid, because I am bringing you some good news. It will be a joy to all the people. ¹¹Today your Savior was born in David's town. He is Christ, the Lord. ¹²This is how you will know him: You will find a baby wrapped in cloths and lying in a feeding box."

¹³Then a very large group of angels from heaven joined the first angel. All the angels were praising God, saying:

¹⁴"Give glory to God in heaven,
    and on earth let there be peace to the people
        who please God."

¹⁵Then the angels left the shepherds and went back to heaven. The shepherds said to each other, "Let us go to Bethlehem and see this thing that has happened. We will see this thing the Lord told us about."

¹⁶So the shepherds went quickly and found Mary and Joseph. ¹⁷And the shepherds saw the baby lying in a feeding box. Then they told what the angels had said about this child. ¹⁸Everyone was amazed when they heard what the shepherds said to them. ¹⁹Mary hid these things in her heart; she continued to think about them. ²⁰Then the shep-

herds went back to their sheep, praising God and thanking him for everything that they had seen and heard. It was just as the angel had told them.

²²The time came for Mary and Joseph to do what the law of Moses taught about being made pure. They took Jesus to Jerusalem to present him to the Lord. ²³It is written in the law of the Lord: "Give every firstborn male to the Lord." ²⁴Mary and Joseph also went to offer a sacrifice, as the law of the Lord says: "You must sacrifice two doves or two young pigeons."

Simeon and Anna Welcome the Lord Jesus

(From Luke 2)

²⁵A man named Simeon lived in Jerusalem. He was a good man and very religious. He was waiting for the time when God would help Israel. The Holy Spirit was in him. ²⁶The Holy Spirit told Simeon that he would not die before he saw the Christ promised by the Lord. ²⁷The Spirit led Simeon to the Temple. Mary and Joseph brought the baby Jesus to the Temple to do what the law said they must do. ²⁸Then Simeon took the baby in his arms and thanked God:

³⁰"I have seen your Salvation with my own eyes.
³¹ You prepared him before all people.
³²He is a light for the non-Jewish people to see.
     He will bring honor to your people, the
     Israelites."

³³Jesus' father and mother were amazed at what Simeon had said about him. ³⁴Then Simeon blessed them and said to Mary, "Many in Israel will fall and many will rise because of this child. He will be a sign from God that many people will not accept. ³⁵The things they think in secret will be made known. And the things that will happen will make your heart sad, too."

³⁶Anna, a prophetess, was there at the Temple. . . . Anna was very old. She had once been married for seven years. ³⁷Then her husband died and she lived alone. She was now 84 years old. Anna never left the Temple. She worshiped God by going without food and praying day and night. ³⁸She was standing there at that time, thanking God. She talked about Jesus to all who were waiting for God to free Jerusalem.

Jesus Visits the Temple with His Parents
(From Luke 2)

2:³⁹ Joseph and Mary . . . went home to Nazareth, their own town in Galilee. ⁴⁰The little child began to grow up. He became stronger and wiser, and God's blessings were with him.

⁴¹Every year Jesus' parents went to Jerusalem for the Passover Feast. ⁴²When Jesus was 12 years old, they went to the feast as they always did. ⁴³When the feast days were over, they went home. The boy Jesus stayed behind in Jerusalem, but his parents did not know it. ⁴⁴Joseph and Mary traveled for a whole day. They thought that Jesus was with them in the group. Then they began to look for him among their family and friends, ⁴⁵but they did not find him. So they went back to Jerusalem to look for him there. ⁴⁶After three days they found him. Jesus was sitting in the Temple with the religious teachers,

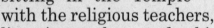

listening to them and asking them questions. ⁴⁷All who heard him were amazed at his understanding and wise answers. ⁴⁸When Jesus' parents saw him, they were amazed. His mother said to him, "Son, why did you do this to us? Your father and I were very worried about you. We have been looking for you."

⁴⁹Jesus asked, "Why did you have to look for me? You should have known that I must be where my Father's work is!" ⁵⁰But they did not understand the meaning of what he said.

⁵¹ᵃJesus went with them to Nazareth and obeyed them. ⁵²Jesus continued to learn more and more

and to grow physically. People liked him, and he pleased God.

John Baptizes the Son of God

(From Luke 3)

3:¹It was the fifteenth year of the rule of Tiberius Caesar. These men were under Caesar: Pontius Pilate was the ruler of Judea. Herod was the ruler of Galilee. Philip, Herod's brother, was the ruler of Iturea and Trachonitis. And Lysanias was the ruler of Abilene. ²Annas and Caiaphas were the high priests. At this time, a command from God came to John son of Zechariah. John was living in the desert. ³He went all over the area around the Jordan River and preached to the people. He preached a baptism of changed hearts and lives for the forgiveness of their sins. ⁴As it is written in the book of Isaiah the prophet:

"This is a voice of a man
   who calls out in the desert:
'Prepare the way for the Lord.
   Make the road straight for him.
⁵Every valley should be filled in.

Every mountain and hill should be made flat.
Roads with turns should be made straight,
    and rough roads should be made smooth.
⁶And all people will know about the salvation of
    God!' "

¹⁵All the people were hoping for the Christ to
come, and they wondered about John. They
thought, "Maybe he is the Christ."

¹⁶John answered everyone, "I baptize you with
water, but there is one coming later who can do
more than I can. I am not good enough to untie his
sandals. He will baptize you with the Holy Spirit
and with fire. ¹⁷He will come ready to clean the
grain. He will separate the good grain from the
chaff. He will put the good part of the grain into
his barn. Then he will burn the chaff with a fire
that cannot be put out." ¹⁸And John continued to
preach the Good News, saying many other things
to encourage the people.

²¹When all the people were being baptized by
John, Jesus was also baptized. While Jesus was
praying, heaven opened and ²²the Holy Spirit came
down on him. The Spirit was in the form of a dove.
Then a voice came from heaven and said, "You are
my Son and I love you. I am very pleased with you."

A Woman Washes Jesus' Feet
(From Luke 7)

7:³⁶ One of the Pharisees asked Jesus to eat with
him. Jesus went into the Pharisee's house and sat

at the table. ³⁷A sinful woman in the town learned that Jesus was eating at the Pharisee's house. So she brought an alabaster jar of perfume. ³⁸She stood at Jesus' feet, crying, and began to wash his feet with her tears. She dried his feet with her hair, kissed them many times and rubbed them with the perfume. ³⁹The Pharisee who asked Jesus to come to his house saw this. He thought to himself, "If Jesus were a prophet, he would know that the woman who is touching him is a sinner!"

⁴⁰Jesus said to the Pharisee, "Simon, I have something to say to you."

Simon said, "Teacher, tell me."

⁴¹Jesus said, "There were two men. Both men owed money to the same banker. One man owed the banker 500 silver coins. The other man owed the banker 50 silver coins. ⁴²The men had no money; so they could not pay what they owed. But the banker told the men that they did not have to pay him. Which one of the two men will love the banker more?"

⁴³Simon, the Pharisee, answered, "I think it would be the one who owed him the most money."

Jesus said to Simon, "You are right." ⁴⁴Then Jesus turned toward the woman and said to Simon, "Do you see this woman? When I came into your house, you gave me no water for my feet. But she washed my feet with her tears and dried my feet with her hair. ⁴⁵You did not kiss me, but she has been kissing my feet since I came in! ⁴⁶You did not rub my head with oil, but she rubbed my feet with perfume. ⁴⁷I tell you that her many sins are forgiven. This is clear because she showed great love. But the person who has only a little to be forgiven will feel only a little love."

⁴⁸Then Jesus said to her, "Your sins are forgiven."

⁴⁹The people sitting at the table began to think to themselves, "Who is this man? How can he forgive sins?"

⁵⁰Jesus said to the woman, "Because you believed, you are saved from your sins. Go in peace."

The Good Samaritan

(From Luke 10)

10:²⁵Then a teacher of the law stood up. He was trying to test Jesus. He said, "Teacher, what must I do to get life forever?"

²⁶Jesus said to him, "What is written in the law? What do you read there?"

²⁷The man answered, "Love the Lord your God. Love him with all your heart, all your soul, all your

strength, and all your mind." Also, "You must love your neighbor as you love yourself."

²⁸Jesus said to him, "Your answer is right. Do this and you will have life forever."

²⁹But the man wanted to show that the way he was living was right. So he said to Jesus, "And who is my neighbor?"

³⁰To answer this question, Jesus said, "A man was going down the road from Jerusalem to Jericho. Some robbers attacked him. They tore off his clothes and beat him. Then they left him lying there, almost dead. ³¹It happened that a Jewish priest was going down that road. When the priest saw the man, he walked by on the other side of the road. ³²Next, a Levite came there. He went over and looked at the man. Then he walked by on the other side of the road. ³³Then a Samaritan traveling down the road came to where the hurt man was lying. He saw the man and felt very sorry for him. ³⁴The Samaritan went to him and poured olive oil and wine on his wounds

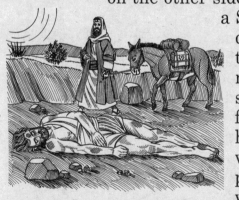

and bandaged them. He put the hurt man on his own donkey and took him to an inn. At the inn, the Samaritan took care of him. ³⁵The next day, the Samaritan brought out two silver coins and gave them to the innkeeper. The Samaritan said, 'Take care of this man. If you spend more money on him, I will pay it back to you when I come again.'"

³⁶Then Jesus said, "Which one of these three men do you think was a neighbor to the man who was attacked by the robbers?"

³⁷The teacher of the law answered, "The one who helped him."

Jesus said to him, "Then go and do the same thing he did!"

Jesus Heals on the Sabbath and Teaches with Stories

(From Luke 13—15)

13:¹⁰ Jesus was teaching in one of the synagogues on the Sabbath day. ¹¹In the synagogue there was a woman who had an evil spirit in her. This spirit had made the woman a cripple for 18 years. Her back was always bent; she could not stand up straight. ¹²When Jesus saw her, he called her over and  said, "Woman, your sickness has left you!" ¹³Jesus put his hands on her. Immediately she was able to stand up straight and began praising God.

¹⁴The synagogue leader was angry because Jesus healed on the Sabbath day. He said to the people,

"There are six days for work. So come to be healed on one of those days. . . . "

¹⁵The Lord answered, "You people are hypocrites! All of you untie your work animals and lead them to drink water every day—even on the Sabbath day! ¹⁶This woman that I healed is our Jewish sister. . . . Surely it is not wrong for her to be freed from her sickness on a Sabbath day!" ¹⁷When Jesus said this, all the men who were criticizing him were ashamed. And all the people were happy for the wonderful things Jesus was doing.

14:¹On a Sabbath day, Jesus went to the home of a leading Pharisee to eat with him. The people there were all watching Jesus very closely. ²A man with dropsy was brought before Jesus. ³Jesus said to the Pharisees and teachers of the law, "Is it right or wrong to heal on the Sabbath day?" ⁴But they would not answer his question. So Jesus took the man, healed him, and sent him away.

15:¹Many tax collectors and "sinners" came to listen to Jesus. ²The Pharisees and the teachers of the law began to complain: "Look! This man welcomes sinners and even eats with them!"

³Then Jesus told them this story: ⁴"Suppose one of you has 100 sheep, but he loses 1 of them. Then he will leave the other 99 sheep alone and go out and look for the lost sheep. The man will keep on searching for the lost sheep until he finds it. ⁵And when he finds it, the man is very happy. He puts it on his shoulders ⁶and goes home. He calls to his friends and neighbors and says, 'Be happy with me because I found my lost sheep!' ⁷In the same way, I tell you

there is much joy in heaven when 1 sinner changes his heart. There is more joy for that 1 sinner than there is for 99 good people who don't need to change.

⁸"Suppose a woman has ten silver coins, but she loses one of them. She will light a lamp and clean the house. She will look carefully for the coin until she finds it. ⁹And when she finds it, she will call her friends and neighbors and say, 'Be happy with me because I have found the coin that I lost!' ¹⁰In the same way, there is joy before the angels of God when 1 sinner changes his heart."

A Son Comes Home
(From Luke 15)

15:¹¹Then Jesus said, "A man had two sons. ¹²The younger son said to the father, 'Give me my share of the property.' So the father divided the property between his two sons. ¹³Then the younger son gathered up all that was his and left. He traveled far away to another country. There he wasted his money in foolish living. ¹⁴ᵇSoon after that, the land became very dry, and there was no rain. There was not enough food to eat anywhere in the country. The son was hungry and needed money. ¹⁵So he got a job . . . feed[ing] pigs. ¹⁶The son was so hungry that he was willing to eat the food the pigs were eating. But no one gave him anything. ¹⁷The son realized that he had been very foolish. He thought, 'All of my father's servants have plenty of food. But I am here, almost dying with hunger. ¹⁸I will leave and return to my father. I'll say to him: Father, I have sinned against God and have done wrong to you. ¹⁹I am not good enough to be called your son. But let me be like one of your servants.' ²⁰So the son left and went to his father.

"While the son was still a long way off, his father saw him coming. He felt sorry for his son. So the father ran to him, and hugged and kissed him. ²¹The son said, 'Father, I have sinned against God and have done wrong to you. I am not good enough to be called your son.' ²²But the father said to his servants, 'Hurry! Bring the best clothes and put them on him. Also, put a ring on his finger and sandals on his feet. ²³And get our fat calf and kill it. Then we can have a feast and celebrate! ²⁴My son was dead, but now he is alive again! He was lost, but now he is found!' So they began to celebrate.

²⁵"The older son was in the field. As he came closer to the house, he heard the sound of music and dancing. ²⁶So he called to one of the servants and asked, 'What does all this mean?' ²⁷The servant said, 'Your brother has come back. Your father killed the fat calf to eat because your brother came home safely!' ²⁸The older son was angry and would not go in to the feast. So his father went out and begged him to come in. ²⁹The son said to his father, 'I have served you like a slave for many years! I have always obeyed your commands. But you never even killed a young goat for me to have a feast with

my friends. ³⁰But your other son has wasted all your money. . . . Then he comes home, and you kill the fat calf for him!' ³¹The father said to him, 'Son, you are always with me. All that I have is yours. ³²We had to celebrate and be happy because your brother was dead, but now he is alive. He was lost, but now he is found.'"

Jesus Helps a Blind Man and Zacchaeus

(From Luke 18 and 19)

18:³⁵Jesus was coming near the city of Jericho. There was a blind man sitting beside the road, begging for money. ³⁶When he heard the people coming down the road, he asked, "What is happening?"

³⁷They told him, "Jesus, the one from Nazareth, is coming here."

³⁸The blind man cried out, "Jesus, Son of David! Please help me!"

³⁹ᵃThe people who were in front, leading the group, told the blind man to be quiet. But the blind man shouted more and more.

⁴⁰Jesus stopped and said, "Bring the blind man to me!" When he came near, Jesus asked him, ⁴¹"What do you want me to do for you?"

He said, "Lord, I want to see again."

⁴²Jesus said to him, "Then see! You are healed because you believed."

⁴³ᵃAt once the man was able to see, and he followed Jesus, thanking God.

19:²In Jericho there was a man named Zacchaeus. He was a wealthy, very important tax collector. ³He wanted to see who Jesus was, but he was too short to see above the crowd. ⁴He ran ahead to a place where he knew Jesus would come. He climbed a sycamore tree so he could see Jesus. ⁵When Jesus came to that place, he looked up and saw Zacchaeus in the tree. He said to him, "Zacchaeus, hurry and come down! I must stay at your house today."

⁶Zacchaeus came down quickly. He was pleased to have Jesus in his house. ⁷All the people saw this and began to complain, "Look at the kind of man Jesus stays with. Zacchaeus is a sinner!"

⁸But Zacchaeus said to the Lord, "I will give half of my money to the poor. If I have cheated anyone, I will pay that person back four times more!"

⁹Jesus said, "Salvation has come to this house today. This man truly belongs to the family of Abraham. ¹⁰The Son of Man came to find lost people and save them."

The Road to Emmaus
(From Luke 24)

24:¹³[After Jesus was crucified and rose from the dead] two of Jesus' followers were going to a town named Emmaus. It is about seven miles from Jerusalem. ¹⁴They were talking about everything that had happened. ¹⁵While they were discussing these things, Jesus himself came near and began walking

with them. ¹⁶(They were not allowed to recognize Jesus.) ¹⁷Then he said, "What are these things you are talking about while you walk?"

The two followers stopped. Their faces were very sad. ¹⁸The one named Cleopas answered, "You must be the only one in Jerusalem who does not know what just happened there."

¹⁹Jesus said to them, "What are you talking about?"

The followers said, "It is about Jesus of Nazareth. He was a prophet from God to all the people. He said and did many powerful things. ²⁰Our leaders and the leading priests gave him up to be judged and killed. They nailed him to a cross. ²¹But we were hoping that he would free the Jews. It is now the third day since this happened. ²²And today some women among us told us some amazing things. Early this morning they went to the tomb, ²³but they did not find his body there. They came and told us that they had seen a vision of angels. The angels said that Jesus was alive! ²⁴So some of our group went to the tomb, too. They found it just as the women said, but they did not see Jesus."

²⁵Then Jesus said to them, "You are foolish and slow to realize what is true. You should believe everything the prophets said. ²⁶They said that the

Christ must suffer these things before he enters his glory." ²⁷Then Jesus began to explain everything that had been written about himself in the Scriptures. He started with Moses, and then he talked about what all the prophets had said about him.

²⁸They came near the town of Emmaus, and Jesus acted as if he did not plan to stop there. ²⁹But they begged him, "Stay with us. It is late; it is almost night." So he went in to stay with them.

³⁰Jesus sat down with them and took some bread. He gave thanks for the food and divided it. Then he gave it to them. ³¹And then, they were allowed to recognize Jesus. But when they saw who he was, he disappeared. ³²They said to each other, "When Jesus talked to us on the road, it felt like a fire burning in us. It was exciting when he explained the true meaning of the Scriptures."

³³So the two followers got up at once and went back to Jerusalem. There they found the 11 apostles and others gathered.

³⁵Then the two followers told what had happened on the road. They talked about how they recognized Jesus when he divided the bread.

Jesus Goes Back to Heaven
(From Luke 24)

24:³⁶While the two followers were telling this, Jesus himself stood among those gathered. He said to them, "Peace be with you."

³⁷They were fearful and terrified. They thought they were seeing a ghost. ³⁸But Jesus said, "Why are you troubled? Why do you doubt what you see? ³⁹Look at my hands and my feet. It is I myself! Touch me. You can see that I have a living body; a ghost does not have a body like this."

⁴⁰After Jesus said this, he showed them his hands and feet. ⁴¹The followers were amazed and very happy. They still could not believe it. Jesus said to them, "Do you have any food here?" ⁴²They gave him a piece of cooked fish. ⁴³While the followers watched, Jesus took the fish and ate it.

⁴⁴He said to them, "Remember when I was with you before? I said that everything written about me must happen—everything in the law of Moses, the books of the prophets, and the Psalms."

⁴⁵Then Jesus opened their minds so they could understand the Scriptures. ⁴⁶He said to them, "It is written that the Christ would be killed and rise from death on the third day. ⁴⁷⁻⁴⁸You saw these things happen—you are witnesses. You must tell people to change their hearts and lives. If they do this, their sins will be forgiven. You must start at Jerusalem and preach these things in my name to all nations. ⁴⁹Listen! My Father has promised you something; I will send it to you. But you must stay in Jerusalem until you have received that power from heaven."

⁵⁰Jesus led his followers out of Jerusalem almost

to Bethany. He raised his hands and blessed them.
⁵¹While he was blessing them, he was separated
from them and carried into heaven. ⁵²They worshiped him and then went back to the city very
happy. ⁵³They stayed in the Temple all the time,
praising God.

Jesus Is the Light of the World

(From John 1)

1:¹Before the world
began, there was the
Word. The Word was
with God, and the Word
was God. ²He was with
God in the beginning.
³All things were made
through him. Nothing
was made without him.

⁴In him there was life. That life was light for the
people of the world. ⁵The Light shines in the darkness. And the darkness has not overpowered the
Light.

⁶There was a man named John who was sent by
God. ⁷He came to tell people about the Light.
Through him all people could hear about the Light
and believe. ⁸John was not the Light, but he came
to tell people about the Light. ⁹The true Light was
coming into the world. The true Light gives light to
all.

¹⁰The Word was in the world. The world was

made through him, but the world did not know him. ¹¹He came to the world that was his own. But his own people did not accept him. ¹²But some people did accept him. They believed in him. To them he gave the right to become children of God. ¹³They did not become his children in the human way. They were not born because of the desire or wish of some man. They were born of God.

¹⁴The Word became a man and lived among us. We saw his glory—the glory that belongs to the only Son of the Father. The Word was full of grace and truth. ¹⁵John told about him. He said, "This is the One I was talking about. I said, 'The One who comes after me is greater than I am. He was living before me.'"

¹⁶The Word was full of grace and truth. From him we all received more and more blessings. ¹⁷The law was given through Moses, but grace and truth came through Jesus Christ. ¹⁸No man has ever seen God. But God the only Son is very close to the Father. And the Son has shown us what God is like.

¹⁹The Jews in Jerusalem sent some priests and Levites to John. The Jews sent them to ask, "Who are you?"

²⁰John spoke freely and did not refuse to answer. He said clearly, "I am not the Christ."

²³John told them in the words of the prophet Isaiah:

"I am the voice of a man
    calling out in the desert:
'Make the road straight for the Lord.'"

²⁴In the group of Jews who were sent, there were

some Pharisees. [25]They said to John: "You say you are not the Christ. . . . Then why do you baptize people?"

[26]John answered, "I baptize people with water. But there is one here with you that you don't know. [27]He is the One who comes after me. I am not good enough to untie the strings of his sandals."

[28]This all happened at Bethany on the other side of the Jordan River. This is where John was baptizing people.

Jesus Chooses Some Followers
(From John 1)

1:[29]The next day John saw Jesus coming toward him. John said, "Look, the Lamb of God. He takes away the sins of the world! [30]This is the One I was talking about. I said, 'A man will come after me, but he is greater than I am, because he was living before me.' [31]Even I did not know who he was. But I came baptizing with water so that the people of Israel could know who he is."

[32-33]Then John said, "I did not know who the Christ was. But God sent me to baptize with water. And God told me, 'You will see the Spirit come down and rest on a man. That man is the One who will baptize with the Holy Spirit.'" John said, "I saw the Spirit come down from heaven. The Spirit looked like a dove and rested on him. [34]I have seen this happen. So I tell people: 'He is the Son of God.'"

³⁵The next day John was there again with two of his followers. ³⁶He saw Jesus walking by and said, "Look, the Lamb of God!"

³⁷The two followers heard John say this. So they followed Jesus. ³⁸Jesus turned and saw them following him. He asked, "What do you want?"

They said, "Rabbi, where are you staying?" ("Rabbi" means "Teacher.")

³⁹Jesus answered, "Come with me and you will see." So the two men went with Jesus. They saw the place where Jesus was staying and stayed there with him that day. It was then about four o'clock.

⁴⁰These two men followed Jesus after they heard about him from John. One of the men was Andrew. He was Simon Peter's brother. ⁴¹The first thing Andrew did was to find his brother, Simon. He said to Simon, "We have found the Messiah." ("Messiah" means "Christ.")

⁴²Then Andrew took Simon to Jesus. Jesus looked at Simon and said, "You are Simon son of John. You will be called Cephas." ("Cephas" means "Peter.")

⁴³The next day Jesus decided to go to Galilee. He found Philip and said to him, "Follow me." ⁴⁴Philip was from the town of Bethsaida, where Andrew and Peter lived. ⁴⁵Philip found Nathanael and told him, "Remember that Moses wrote in the law about a man who was coming, and the prophets also wrote about him. We have found

248

him. He is Jesus, the son of Joseph. He is from Nazareth."

⁴⁶But Nathanael said to Philip, "Nazareth! Can anything good come from Nazareth?"

Philip answered, "Come and see."

⁴⁷Jesus saw Nathanael coming toward him. He said, "Here is truly a person of Israel. There is nothing false in him."

⁴⁸Nathanael asked, "How do you know me?"

Jesus answered, "I saw you when you were under the fig tree. That was before Philip told you about me."

⁴⁹Then Nathanael said to Jesus, "Teacher, you are the Son of God. You are the King of Israel."

⁵⁰Jesus said to Nathanael, "You believe in me because I told you I saw you under the fig tree. But you will see greater things than that!" ⁵¹And Jesus said to them, "I tell you the truth. You will all see heaven open. You will see 'angels of God going up and coming down' on the Son of Man."

The Wedding at Cana
(From John 2)

2:¹Two days later there was a wedding in the town of Cana in Galilee. Jesus' mother was there. ²Jesus and his followers were also invited to the wedding. ³When all the wine was gone, Jesus' mother said to him, "They have no more wine."

⁴Jesus answered, "Dear woman, why come to me? My time has not yet come."

⁵His mother said to the servants, "Do whatever he tells you to do."

⁶In that place there were six stone water jars. The Jews used jars like these in their washing ceremony. Each jar held about 20 or 30 gallons.

⁷Jesus said to the servants, "Fill the jars with water." So they filled the jars to the top.

⁸Then he said to them, "Now take some out and give it to the master of the feast."

So the servants took the water to the master. ⁹When he tasted it, the water had become wine. He did not know where the wine came from. But the servants who brought the water knew. The master of the wedding called the bridegroom ¹⁰and said to him, "People always serve the best wine first. Later, after the guests have been drinking a lot, they serve the cheaper wine. But you have saved the best wine till now."

¹¹So in Cana of Galilee, Jesus did his first miracle. There he showed his glory, and his followers believed in him.

Jesus Cleanses the Temple in Jerusalem

(From John 2)

2:¹² Then Jesus went to the town of Capernaum with his mother, brothers and his followers. They all stayed in Capernaum for a few days. ¹³But it was almost time for the Jewish Passover Feast. So Jesus went to Jerusalem. ¹⁴In the Temple he found men selling cattle, sheep, and doves. He saw others sitting at tables, exchanging

money. ¹⁵Jesus made a whip out of cords. Then he forced all these men, with the sheep and cattle, to leave the Temple. He turned over the tables and scattered the money of the men who were exchanging it. ¹⁶Then he said to those who were selling pigeons, "Take these things out of here! Don't make my Father's house a place for buying and selling!"

¹⁷When this happened the followers remembered what was written in the Scriptures: "My strong love for your Temple completely controls me."

¹⁸The Jews said to Jesus, "Show us a miracle for a sign. Prove that you have the right to do these things."

¹⁹Jesus answered, "Destroy this temple, and I will build it again in three days."

²⁰The Jews answered, "Men worked 46 years to build this Temple! Do you really believe you can build it again in three days?"

²¹(But the temple Jesus meant was his own body. ²²After Jesus was raised from death, his followers remembered that Jesus had said this. Then they believed the Scripture and the words Jesus said.)

²³Jesus was in Jerusalem for the Passover Feast. Many people believed in him because they saw the miracles he did.

Nicodemus Visits Jesus

(From John 3)

3:¹There was a man named Nicodemus who was one of the Pharisees. He was an important Jewish leader. ²One night Nicodemus came to Jesus. He said, "Teacher, we know that you are a teacher sent from God. No one can do the miracles you do, unless God is with him."

³Jesus answered, "I tell you the truth. Unless one is born again, he cannot be in God's kingdom."

⁴Nicodemus said, "But if a man is already old, how can he be born again? He cannot enter his mother's body again. So how can he be born a second time?"

⁵But Jesus answered, "I tell you the truth. Unless one is born from water and the Spirit, he cannot enter God's kingdom. ⁶A person's body is born from his human parents. But a person's spiritual life is born from the Spirit. ⁷Don't be surprised when I tell you, 'You must all be born again.' ⁸The wind blows where it wants to go. You hear the wind blow. But you don't know where the wind comes from or where it is going. It is the same with every person who is born from the Spirit."

⁹Nicodemus asked, "How can all this be possible?"

¹⁰Jesus said, "You are an important teacher in Israel. But you still don't understand these things?

¹¹I tell you the truth. We talk about what we know. We tell about what we have seen. But you don't accept what we tell you. ¹²I have told you about things here on earth, but you do not believe me. So surely you will not believe me if I tell you about the things of heaven! ¹³The only one who has ever gone up to heaven is the One who came down from heaven—the Son of Man.

¹⁴"Moses lifted up the snake in the desert. It is the same with the Son of Man. The Son of Man must be lifted up too. ¹⁵Then everyone who believes in him can have eternal life.

¹⁶"For God loved the world so much that he gave his only Son. God gave his Son so that whoever believes in him may not be lost, but have eternal life. ¹⁷God did not send his Son into the world to judge the world guilty, but to save the world through him. ¹⁸He who believes in God's Son is not judged guilty. He who does not believe has already been judged guilty, because he has not believed in God's only Son. ¹⁹People are judged by this fact: I am the Light from God that has come into the world. But men did not want light. They wanted darkness because they were doing evil things. ²⁰Everyone who does evil hates the light. He will not come to the light because it will show all the evil things he has done. ²¹But he who follows the true way comes to the light. Then the light will show that the things he has done were done through God."

The Woman at the Well

(From John 4)

4:³So [Jesus] left Judea and went back to Galilee. ⁴On the way he had to go through the country of Samaria.

⁵In Samaria Jesus came to the town called Sychar. This town is near the field that Jacob gave to his son Joseph. ⁶Jacob's well was there. Jesus was tired from his long trip. So he sat down beside the well. It was about noon. ⁷A Samaritan woman came to the well to get some water. Jesus said to her, "Please give me a drink." ⁸(This happened while Jesus' followers were in town buying some food.)

⁹The woman said, "I am surprised that you ask me for a drink. You are a Jew and I am a Samaritan." (Jews are not friends with Samaritans.)

¹⁰Jesus said, "You don't know what God gives. And you don't know who asked you for a drink. If you knew, you would have asked me, and I would have given you living water."

¹¹The woman said, "Sir, where will you get that living water? The well is very deep, and you have nothing to get water with. ¹²Are you greater than Jacob, our father? Jacob is the one who gave us this well. He drank from it himself. Also, his sons and flocks drank from this well."

¹³Jesus answered, "Every person who drinks this water will be thirsty again. ¹⁴But whoever drinks the water I give will never be thirsty again. The water I give will become a spring of water flowing inside him. It will give him eternal life."

¹⁵The woman said to him, "Sir, give me this water. Then I will never be thirsty again. And I will not have to come back here to get more water."

¹⁶Jesus told her, "Go get your husband and come back here."

¹⁷The woman answered, "But I have no husband."

Jesus said to her, "You are right to say you have no husband. ¹⁸Really you have had five husbands. But the man you live with now is not your husband. You told the truth."

¹⁹The woman said, "Sir, I can see that you are a prophet. ²⁰Our fathers worshiped on this mountain. But you Jews say that Jerusalem is the place where people must worship."

²¹Jesus said, "Believe me, woman. The time is coming when you will not have to be in Jerusalem or on this mountain to worship the Father. ²²You Samaritans worship what you don't understand. We Jews understand what we worship. Salvation comes from the Jews. ²³The time is coming when the true worshipers will worship the Father in spirit and truth. That time is now here. And these are the kinds of worshipers the Father wants. ²⁴God is spirit. Those who worship God must worship in spirit and truth."

²⁵The woman said, "I know that the Messiah is coming." (Messiah is the One called Christ.) "When

the Messiah comes, he will explain everything to us."

²⁶Then Jesus said, "He is talking to you now. I am he."

Jesus Heals an Officer's Son and a Lame Man

(From John 4 and 5)

4:⁴⁶Jesus went to visit Cana in Galilee again. This is where Jesus had changed the water into wine. One of the king's important officers lived in the city of Capernaum. This man's son was sick. ⁴⁷The man heard that Jesus had come from Judea and was now in Galilee. He went to Jesus and begged him to come to Capernaum and heal his son. His son was almost dead. ⁴⁸Jesus said to him, "You people must see signs and miracles before you will believe in me."

⁴⁹The officer said, "Sir, come before my child dies."

⁵⁰Jesus answered, "Go. Your son will live."

The man believed what Jesus told him and went home. ⁵¹On the way the man's servants came and met him. They told him, "Your son is well."

⁵²The man asked, "What time did my son begin to get well?"

They answered, "It was about one o'clock yesterday when the fever left him."

⁵³The father knew that one o'clock was the exact time that Jesus had said, "Your son will live." So

the man and all the people of his house believed in Jesus.

5:[1]Later Jesus went to Jerusalem for a special Jewish feast. [2]In Jerusalem there is a pool with five covered porches. In the Jewish language it is called Bethzatha. This pool is near the Sheep Gate. [3]Many sick people were lying on the porches beside the pool. Some were blind, some were crippled, and some were paralyzed. [5]There was a man lying there who had been sick for 38 years. [6]Jesus saw the man and knew that he had been sick for a very long time. So Jesus asked him, "Do you want to be well?"

[7]The sick man answered, "Sir, there is no one to help me get into the pool when the water starts moving. I try to be the first one into the water. But when I try, someone else always goes in before I can."

[8]Then Jesus said, "Stand up. Pick up your mat and walk." [9]And immediately the man was well. He picked up his mat and began to walk.

The day all this happened was a Sabbath day. [10]So the Jews said to the man who had been healed, "Today is the Sabbath. It is against our law for you to carry your mat on the Sabbath day."

[11]But he answered, "The man who made me well told me, 'Pick up your mat and walk.'"

[12]Then they asked him, "Who is the man who told you to pick up your mat and walk?"

[13]But the man who had been healed did not know who it was. There were many people in that place, and Jesus had left.

[14]Later, Jesus found the man at the Temple. Jesus said to him, "See, you are well now. But stop sinning or something worse may happen to you!"

[15]Then the man left and went back to the Jews. He told them that Jesus was the one who had made him well.

Jesus Heals a Man Born Blind
(From John 9)

9:[1]As Jesus was walking along, he saw a man who had been born blind. [2]His followers asked him, "Teacher, whose sin caused this man to be born blind—his own sin or his parents' sin?"

[3]Jesus answered, "It is not this man's sin or his parents' sin that made him be blind. This man was born blind so that God's power could be shown in him."

[6]After Jesus said this, he spit on the ground and made some mud with it. He put the mud on the man's eyes. [7]Then he told the man, "Go and wash in the Pool of Siloam." (Siloam means Sent.) So the man went to the pool. He washed and came back. And he was able to see.

[8]Some people had seen this man begging before. They and the man's neighbors said, "Look! Is this the same man who always sits and begs?"

[9]Some said, "Yes! He is the one." But others said,

"No, he's not the same man. He only looks like him."

So the man himself said, "I am the man."

¹⁰They asked, "What happened? How did you get your sight?"

¹¹He answered, "The man named Jesus made some mud and put it on my eyes. Then he told me to go to Siloam and wash. So I went and washed and came back seeing."

¹²They asked him, "Where is this man?"

The man answered, "I don't know."

¹³Then the people took to the Pharisees the man who had been blind. ¹⁴The day Jesus had made mud and healed his eyes was a Sabbath day. ¹⁵So now the Pharisees asked the man, "How did you get your sight?"

He answered, "He put mud on my eyes. I washed, and now I can see."

¹⁶Some of the Pharisees were saying, "This man does not keep the Sabbath day. He is not from God!"

Others said, "But a man who is a sinner can't do miracles like these." So they could not agree with each other.

¹⁸The Jews did not believe that he had been blind and could now see again. So they sent for the man's parents ¹⁹and asked them, "Is this your son? You say that he was born blind. Then how does he see now?"

²⁰His parents answered, "We know that this is our son, and we know that he was born blind. ²¹But we

don't know how he can see now. We don't know who opened his eyes. Ask him. He is old enough to answer for himself." [22]His parents said this because they were afraid of the Jews. The Jews had already decided that anyone who said that Jesus was the Christ would be put out of the synagogue.

[24]So for the second time, they called the man who had been blind. They said, "You should give God the glory by telling the truth. We know that [Jesus] is a sinner."

[25]He answered, "I don't know if he is a sinner. But one thing I do know. I was blind, and now I can see."

Lazarus, Come Out!
(From John 11)

11:[1]There was a man named Lazarus who was sick. He lived in the town of Bethany, where Mary and her sister Martha lived. [2a]Mary is the woman who later put perfume on the Lord and wiped his feet with her hair. [3]So Mary and Martha sent someone to tell Jesus, "Lord, the one you love is sick."

[4]When Jesus heard this he said, "This sickness will not end in death. . . . This has happened to bring glory to the Son of God." [5]Jesus loved Martha and her sister and Lazarus. [6]But when he heard that Lazarus was sick, he stayed where he was for two more days. [7]Then Jesus said to his followers, "Let us go back to Judea."

[17]Jesus arrived in Bethany. There he learned that

Lazarus had already been dead and in the tomb for four days.

²⁰Martha heard that Jesus was coming, and she went out to meet him. But Mary stayed at home. ²¹Martha said to Jesus, "Lord, if you had been here, my brother would not have died. ²²But I know that even now God will give you anything you ask."

²⁵Jesus said to her, "I am the resurrection and the life. He who believes in me will have life even if he dies. ²⁶And he who lives and believes in me will never die. Martha, do you believe this?"

²⁷Martha answered, "Yes, Lord. I believe that you are the Christ, the Son of God. You are the One who was coming to the world."

²⁸[Martha] went back to her sister Mary. . . . Martha said, "The Teacher is here and he is asking for you." ²⁹When Mary heard this, she got up quickly and went to Jesus. ³⁰Jesus had not yet come into the town. ³² . . . Mary went to the place where Jesus was. When she saw him, she fell at his feet and said, "Lord, if you had been here, my brother would not have died."

³³Jesus saw that Mary was crying. . . . Jesus felt very sad in his heart and was deeply troubled. ³⁴He asked, "Where did you bury him?"

"Come and see, Lord," they said.

³⁵Jesus cried.

³⁶So the Jews said, "See how much he loved him."

³⁷But some of them said, "If Jesus healed the eyes of the blind man, why didn't he keep Lazarus from dying?"

³⁸Again Jesus felt very sad in his heart. He came to the tomb. The tomb was a cave with a large stone

covering the entrance. ³⁹ᵃJesus said, "Move the stone away."

⁴¹So they moved the stone away from the entrance. Then Jesus looked up and said, "Father, I thank you that you heard me. ⁴²I know that you always hear me. But I said these things because of the people here around me. I want them to believe that you sent me." ⁴³After Jesus said this, he cried out in a loud voice, "Lazarus, come out!" ⁴⁴The dead man came out. His hands and feet were wrapped with pieces of cloth, and he had a cloth around his face.

Jesus said to them, "Take the cloth off of him and let him go."

The Leaders Plan to Kill Jesus
(From John 11 and 12)

11:⁴⁵There were many Jews who had come to visit Mary. They saw what Jesus did. And many of

them believed in him. ⁴⁶But some of them went to the Pharisees. They told the Pharisees what Jesus had done. ⁴⁷Then the leading priests and Pharisees called a meeting of the Jewish council. They asked, "What should we do? This man is doing many miracles. ⁴⁸If we let him continue doing these things, everyone will believe in him. Then the Romans will come and take away our Temple and our nation."

⁵³That day they started planning to kill Jesus.

⁵⁵It was almost time for the Jewish Passover Feast. Many from the country went up to Jerusalem before the Passover. They went to do the special things to make themselves pure. ⁵⁶The people looked for Jesus. They stood in the Temple and were asking each other, "Is he coming to the Feast?

What do you think?" ⁵⁷But the leading priests and the Pharisees had given orders about Jesus. They said that if anyone knew where Jesus was, he must tell them. Then they could arrest Jesus.

12:¹Six days before the Passover Feast, Jesus went to Bethany, where Lazarus lived. (Lazarus is the man Jesus raised from death.) ²There they had a dinner for Jesus. Martha served the food. Lazarus was one of the people eating with Jesus. ³Mary brought in a pint of very expensive perfume made from pure nard. She poured the perfume on Jesus' feet, and then she wiped his feet with her hair. And the sweet smell from the perfume filled the whole house.

⁴Judas Iscariot, one of Jesus' followers, was there. (He was the one who would later turn against Jesus.) Judas said, ⁵"This perfume was worth 300 silver coins. It should have been sold and the money given to the poor." ⁶But Judas did not really care about the poor. He said this because he was a thief. He was the one who kept the money box, and he often stole money from it.

⁷Jesus answered, "Let her alone. It was right for her to save this perfume for today—the day for me to be prepared for burial. ⁸The poor will always be with you, but you will not always have me."

⁹A large crowd of Jews heard that Jesus was in Bethany. So they went there to see not only Jesus but also Lazarus. Lazarus was the one Jesus raised from death. ¹⁰So the leading priests made plans to kill Lazarus, too. ¹¹Because of Lazarus many Jews were leaving them and believing in Jesus.

¹²The next day a great crowd in Jerusalem heard that Jesus was coming there. These were the people who had come to the Passover Feast. ¹³They took branches of palm trees and went out to meet Jesus. They shouted,

"Praise God!

God bless the One who comes in the name of the Lord!

God bless the King of Israel!"

¹⁹So the Pharisees said to each other, "You can see that nothing is going right for us. Look! The whole world is following him."

Jesus Washes His Followers' Feet

(From John 13)

13:¹It was almost time for the Jewish Passover Feast. Jesus knew that it was time for him to leave this world and go back to the Father. He had always loved those who were his own in the world, and he loved them all the way to the end.

²ᵃJesus and his followers were at the evening meal. The devil had already persuaded Judas Iscariot to turn against Jesus. ³Jesus knew that the Father had given him power over everything. He also knew that he had come from God and was going back to God. ⁴So during the meal Jesus stood

up and took off his outer clothing. Taking a towel, he wrapped it around his waist. [5]Then he poured water into a bowl and began to wash the followers' feet. He dried them with the towel that was wrapped around him.

[6]Jesus came to Simon Peter. But Peter said to Jesus, "Lord, are you going to wash my feet?"

[7]Jesus answered, "You don't understand what I am doing now. But you will understand later."

[8]Peter said, "No! You will never wash my feet."

Jesus answered, "If I don't wash your feet, then you are not one of my people."

[9]Simon Peter answered, "Lord, after you wash my feet, wash my hands and my head, too!"

[10]Jesus said, "After a person has had a bath, his whole body is clean. He needs only to wash his feet. And you men are clean, but not all of you." [11]Jesus knew who would turn against him. That is why Jesus said, "Not all of you are clean."

[12]When he had finished washing their feet, he put on his clothes and sat down again. Jesus asked, "Do you understand what I have just done for you? [13]You call me 'Teacher' and 'Lord.' And this is right, because that is what I am. [14]I, your Lord and Teacher, have washed your feet. So you also should wash each other's feet. [15]I did this as an example for you. So you should do as I have done for you. [16]I tell you the truth. A servant is not greater than his master. A messenger is not greater than the one who sent him. [17]If you know these things, you will be happy if you do them.

[18]"I am not talking about all of you. I know those I have chosen. But what the Scripture said must

happen: 'The man who ate at my table has now turned against me.' [19]I am telling you this now before it happens. Then when it happens you will believe that I am he. [20]I tell you the truth. Whoever accepts anyone I send also accepts me. And whoever accepts me also accepts the One who sent me."

[33a]Jesus said, "My children, I will be with you only a little longer.

[34]"I give you a new command: Love each other. You must love each other as I have loved you. [35]All people will know that you are my followers if you love each other."

Jesus Is Arrested

(From John 18 and 19)

18:[1b]They [Jesus and his followers] went across the Kidron Valley. On the other side there was a garden of olive trees. Jesus and his followers went there.

[2]Judas knew where this place was, because Jesus met there often with his followers. Judas was the one who turned against Jesus. [3]So Judas led a group of soldiers to the garden. Judas also brought some guards from the leading priests and the Pharisees. They were carrying torches, lanterns, and weapons.

[4]Jesus knew everything that would happen to him. Jesus went out and asked, "Who is it you are looking for?"

⁵The men answered, "Jesus from Nazareth."

Jesus said, "I am Jesus." (Judas, the one who turned against Jesus, was standing there with them.) ⁶When Jesus said, "I am Jesus," the men moved back and fell to the ground.

⁷Jesus asked them again, "Who is it you are looking for?"

They said, "Jesus of Nazareth."

⁸Jesus said, "I told you that I am he. So if you are looking for me, then let these other men go." ⁹This happened so that the words Jesus said before might come true: "I have not lost any of the men you gave me."

¹⁰Simon Peter had a sword. He took out the sword and struck the servant of the high priest, cutting off his right ear. (The servant's name was Malchus.) ¹¹Jesus said to Peter, "Put your sword back. Shall I not drink of the cup the Father has given me?"

¹²Then the soldiers with their commander and the Jewish guards arrested Jesus. They tied him ¹³and led him first to Annas. Annas was the father-in-law of Caiaphas, the high priest that year.

²⁴Then Annas sent Jesus to Caiphas, the high priest. Jesus was still tied.

²⁸ᵃThen they led Jesus from Caiaphas' house to the Roman governor's palace. It was early in the morning. ²⁹So Pilate . . . asked, "What charges do you bring against this man?"

³⁰They answered, "He is a criminal. That is why we brought him to you."

268

³⁸Pilate said, . . . "I can find nothing to charge against this man. ³⁹But it is your custom that I free one prisoner to you at the time of the Passover. Do you want me to free this 'king of the Jews'?"

⁴⁰They shouted back, "No, not him! Let Barabbas go free!" (Barabbas was a robber.)

19:¹Then Pilate ordered that Jesus be taken away and whipped. ²The soldiers used some thorny branches to make a crown. They put this crown on Jesus' head and put a purple robe around him. ³Then they came to Jesus many times and said, "Hail, King of the Jews!" They hit Jesus in the face.

⁴Again Pilate came out and said to them, "Look! I am bringing Jesus out to you. I want you to know that I find nothing I can charge against him."

⁶When the leading priests and the guards saw Jesus they shouted, "Kill him on a cross! Kill him on a cross!"

¹⁶So Pilate gave Jesus to them to be killed on a cross.

Jesus on the Cross
(From John 19)

19:¹⁶ᵇThe soldiers took charge of Jesus. ¹⁷Carrying his own cross, Jesus went out to a place called The Place of the Skull. (In the Jewish language this place is called Golgotha.) ¹⁸There they nailed Jesus to the cross. They also put two other men on crosses, one on each side of Jesus with Jesus in the middle. [19]Pilate wrote a sign and put it on the cross. It read: "JESUS OF NAZARETH, THE KING OF THE JEWS." [21]The leading Jewish priests said to Pilate, "Don't write, 'The King of Jews.' But write, 'This man said, I am the King of the Jews.'"

[22]Pilate answered, "What I have written, I have written!"

[23]After the soldiers nailed Jesus to the cross, they took his clothes. They divided them into four parts. Each soldier got one part. They also took his long shirt. It was all one piece of cloth, woven from top to bottom. [24]So the soldiers said to each other, "We should not tear this into parts. We should throw lots to see who will get it." This happened to give full meaning to the Scripture:

"They divided my clothes among them.
And they threw lots for my clothing."

So the soldiers did this.

[25]Jesus' mother stood near his cross. His mother's sister was also standing there, with Mary the wife of Clopas, and Mary Magdalene. [26]Jesus saw his mother. He also saw the follower he loved standing there. He said to his mother, "Dear woman, here is your son." [27]Then he said to the follower, "Here is your mother." From that time on, this follower took her to live in his home.

[28]After this, Jesus knew that everything had been done. To make the Scripture come true, he said, "I am thirsty." [29]There was a jar full of vinegar there,

so the soldiers soaked a sponge in it. Then they put the sponge on a branch of a hyssop plant and lifted it to Jesus' mouth. [30]Jesus tasted the vinegar. Then he said, "It is finished." He bowed his head and died.

[31]This day was Preparation Day. The next day was a special Sabbath day. The Jews did not want the bodies to stay on the cross on the Sabbath day. So they asked Pilate to order that the legs of the men be broken and the bodies be taken away. [32]So the soldiers came and broke the legs of the first man on the cross beside Jesus. Then they broke the legs of the man on the other cross beside Jesus. [33]But when the soldiers came to Jesus, they saw that he was already dead. So they did not break his legs. [34]But one of the soldiers stuck his spear into Jesus' side. At once blood and water came out. [36]These things happened to make the Scripture come true: "Not one of his bones will be broken." [37]And another Scripture said, "They will look at the one they have stabbed."

The Empty Tomb
(From John 19 and 20)

19:[38]Later, a man named Joseph from Arimathea asked Pilate if he could take the body of Jesus. (Joseph was a secret follower of Jesus, because he was afraid of the Jews.) Pilate gave his permission. So Joseph came and took Jesus' body away. [39]Nicodemus went with Joseph. Nicodemus was the man who earlier had come to Jesus at night. He brought about 75 pounds of spices. This was a mixture of myrrh and aloes. ⁴⁰These two men took Jesus' body and wrapped it with the spices in pieces of linen cloth. (This is how the Jews bury people.) ⁴¹In the place where Jesus was killed, there was a garden. In the garden was a new tomb where no one had ever been buried. ⁴²The men laid Jesus in that tomb because it was near, and the Jews were preparing to start their Sabbath day.

20:¹Early on the first day of the week, Mary Magdalene went to the tomb. It was still dark.

Mary saw that the large stone had been moved away from the tomb. ²So Mary ran to Simon Peter and the other follower (the one Jesus loved). Mary said, "They have taken the Lord out of the tomb. We don't know where they have put him."

³So Peter and the other follower started for the tomb. ⁴They were both running, but the other follower ran faster than Peter. So the other follower reached the tomb first. ⁵He bent down and looked in. He saw the strips of linen cloth lying there, but he did not go in. ⁶Then following him came Simon Peter. He went into the

tomb and saw the strips of linen lying there. ⁷He also saw the cloth that had been around Jesus' head. The cloth was folded up and laid in a different place from the strips of linen. ⁸Then the other follower, who had reached the tomb first, also went in. He saw and believed. ⁹(These followers did not yet understand from the Scriptures that Jesus must rise from death.)

¹⁰Then the followers went back home. ¹¹But Mary stood outside the tomb, crying. While she was still crying, she bent down and looked inside the tomb. ¹²She saw two angels dressed in white. They were sitting where Jesus' body had been, one at the head and one at the feet.

¹³They asked her, "Woman, why are you crying?"

She answered, "They have taken away my Lord. I don't know where they have put him." ¹⁴When Mary said this, she turned around and saw Jesus standing there. But she did not know that it was Jesus.

¹⁵Jesus asked her, "Woman, why are you crying? Whom are you looking for?"

Mary thought he was the gardener. So she said to him, "Did you take him away, sir? Tell me where you put him, and I will get him."

¹⁶Jesus said to her, "Mary."

Mary turned toward Jesus and said in the Jewish language, "Rabboni." (This means Teacher.)

¹⁷Jesus said to her, "Don't hold me. I have not yet gone up to the Father. But go to my brothers and tell them this: 'I am going back to my Father and your Father. I am going back to my God and your God.'"

¹⁸Mary Magdalene went and said to the followers, "I saw the Lord!" And she told them what Jesus had said to her.

Jesus Appears to His Followers

(From John 20 and 21)

20:¹⁹It was the first day of the week. That evening the followers were together. The doors were locked, because they were afraid of the Jews. Then Jesus came and stood among them. He said, "Peace be with you!" ²⁰After he said this, he showed them his hands and his side. The followers were very happy when they saw the Lord.

²¹Then Jesus said again, "Peace be with you! As the Father sent me, I now send you." ²²After he said this, he breathed on them and said, "Receive the Holy Spirit. ²³If you forgive anyone his sins, they are forgiven. If you don't forgive them, they are not forgiven."

²⁴Thomas . . . was not with the followers when Jesus came. Thomas was 1 of the 12. ²⁵The other followers told Thomas, "We saw the Lord."

But Thomas said, "I will not believe it until I see the nail marks in his hands. And I will not believe until I put my finger where the nails were and put my hand into his side."

²⁶A week later the follow-

ers were in the house again. Thomas was with them. The doors were locked, but Jesus came in and stood among them. He said, "Peace be with you!" 27Then he said to Thomas, "Put your finger here. Look at my hands. Put your hand here in my side. Stop doubting and believe."

28Thomas said to him, "My Lord and my God!"

29Then Jesus told him, "You believe because you see me. Those who believe without seeing me will be truly happy."

21:1aLater, Jesus showed himself to his followers by Lake Galilee. 2aSome of the followers were together. 3Simon Peter said, "I am going out to fish."

The other followers said, "We will go with you." So they went out and got into the boat. They fished that night but caught nothing.

4Early the next morning Jesus stood on the shore. But the followers did not know that it was Jesus. 5Then he said to them, "Friends, have you caught any fish?"

They answered, "No."

6He said, "Throw your net into the water on the right side of the boat, and you will find some." So they did this. They caught so many fish that they could not pull the net back into the boat.

7The follower whom Jesus loved said to Peter, "It is the Lord!" When Peter heard him say this, he wrapped his coat around himself. (Peter had taken his clothes off.) Then he jumped into the water. 8aThe other followers went to shore in the boat, dragging the net full of fish. 9When the followers stepped out of the boat and onto the shore, they saw a fire of hot coals. There were fish on the fire, and there was bread.

[12]Jesus said to them, "Come and eat." None of the followers dared ask him, "Who are you?" They knew it was the Lord. [13]Jesus came and took the bread and gave it to them. He also gave them the fish.

Jesus' Followers Wait Together
(From Acts 1)

1:[2]I [Luke] wrote about the whole life of Jesus, from the beginning until the day he was taken up into heaven. Before this, Jesus talked to the apostles he had chosen. With the help of the Holy Spirit, Jesus told them what they should do. [3]After his death, he showed himself to them and proved in many ways that he was alive. The apostles saw Jesus during the 40 days after he was raised from death. He spoke to them about the kingdom of God. [4]Once when he was eating with them, he told them not to leave Jerusalem. He said, "The Father has made you a promise which I told you about before. Wait here to receive this promise. [5]John baptized people with water, but in a few days you will be baptized with the Holy Spirit."

[6]The apostles were all together. They asked Jesus, "Lord, are you at this time going to give the kingdom back to Israel?"

[7]Jesus said to them, "The Father is the only One who has the authority to decide dates and times.

These things are not for you to know. ⁸But the Holy Spirit will come to you. Then you will receive power. You will be my witnesses—in Jerusalem, in all of Judea, in Samaria, and in every part of the world."

⁹After he said this, as they were watching, he was lifted up. A cloud hid him from their sight. ¹⁰As he was going, they were looking into the sky. Suddenly, two men wearing white clothes stood beside them. ¹¹They said, "Men of Galilee, why are you standing here looking into the sky? You saw Jesus taken away from you into heaven. He will come back in the same way you saw him go."

¹²ᵃThen they went back to Jerusalem from the Mount of Olives. ¹³ᵃWhen they entered the city, they went to the upstairs room where they were staying. ¹⁴They all continued praying together. Some women, including Mary the mother of Jesus, and Jesus' brothers were also there with the apostles.

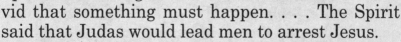

¹⁵ᵇPeter stood up and said, ¹⁶⁻¹⁷"Brothers, in the Scriptures the Holy Spirit said through David that something must happen. . . . The Spirit said that Judas would lead men to arrest Jesus.

²¹⁻²²"So now a man must join us and become a witness of Jesus' being raised from death. He must be one of the men who were part of our group during all the time the Lord Jesus was with us . . . until the day when Jesus was taken up from us to heaven."

²³They put the names of two men before the

group. One was Joseph Barsabbas, who was also called Justus. The other was Matthias. ^{24–25}The apostles prayed, "Lord, you know the minds of everyone. Show us which one of these two you have chosen to do this work. . . . " ²⁶Then they used lots to choose between them, and the lots showed that Matthias was the one. So he became an apostle with the other 11.

The Coming of the Holy Spirit

(From Acts 2)

2:¹When the day of Pentecost came, [the followers of Jesus] were all together in one place. ²Suddenly a noise came from heaven. It sounded like a strong wind blowing. This noise filled the whole house where they were sitting. ³They saw something that looked like flames of fire. The flames were separated and stood over each person there. ⁴They were

all filled with the Holy Spirit, and they began to speak different languages. The Holy Spirit was giving them the power to speak these languages.

⁵There were some religious Jews staying in Jerusalem who were from every country in the world. ⁶When they heard this noise, a crowd came together. They were all surprised, because each one heard them speaking in his own language. ⁷They were completely amazed at this. They said, "Look! Aren't all these men that we hear speaking from Galilee? ⁸But each of us hears them in his own language. How is this possible? We are from different places: ¹¹ᵇBut we hear these men telling in our own languages about the great things God has done!" ¹²They were all amazed and confused. They asked each other, "What does this mean?"

¹³But others were making fun of them, saying, "They have had too much wine."

¹⁴But Peter stood up with the 11 apostles. In a loud voice he spoke to the crowd: "My fellow Jews, and all of you who are in Jerusalem, listen to me. Pay attention to what I have to say. ¹⁵These men are not drunk, as you think; it is only nine o'clock in the morning! ¹⁶But Joel the prophet wrote about what is happening here today:

¹⁷"God says: In the last days
I will give my Spirit freely to all kinds of people.
Your sons and daughters will prophesy.
Your old men will dream dreams.
Your young men will see visions.
¹⁸At that time I will give my Spirit
even to my servants, both men and women.
And they will prophesy.'

²²"Men of Israel, listen to these words: Jesus from Nazareth was a very special man. God clearly showed this to you by the miracles, wonders, and signs God did through him. You all know this, because it happened right here among you. ²³Jesus was given to you, and you killed him. But God knew all this would happen. This was God's plan which he had made long ago. ²⁴God raised Jesus from death. God set him free from the pain of death. Death could not hold him.

³²"So Jesus is the One who God raised from death! And we are all witnesses to this. ³³Jesus was lifted up to heaven and is now at God's right side. The Father has given the Holy Spirit to Jesus as he promised. So now Jesus has poured out that Spirit. This is what you see and hear."

⁴¹Then those people who accepted what Peter said were baptized. About 3,000 people were added to the number of believers that day.

Peter Heals a Crippled Man

(From Acts 3 and 4)

3:¹One day Peter and John went to the Temple. It was three o'clock in the afternoon. This was the time for the daily prayer service. ²There, at the Temple gate called Beautiful Gate, was a man who had been crippled all his life. Every day he was carried to this gate to beg. He would ask for money from the people going into the Temple. ³The man saw Peter and John going into the Temple and

asked them for money. [4]Peter and John looked straight at him and said, "Look at us!" [5]The man looked at them; he thought they were going to give him some money. [6]But Peter said, "I don't have any silver or gold, but I do have something else I can give you: By the power of Jesus Christ from Nazareth—stand up and walk!" [7]Then Peter took the man's right hand and lifted him up. Immediately the man's feet and ankles became strong. [8]He jumped up, stood on his feet, and began to walk. He went into the Temple with them, walking and jumping, and praising God. [9-10]All the people recognized him. They knew he was the crippled man who always sat by the Beautiful Gate begging for money. Now they saw this same man walking and praising God. The people were amazed. They could not understand how this could happen.

¹¹The man was holding on to Peter and John. All the people were amazed and ran to Peter and John at Solomon's Porch. ¹²When Peter saw this, he said to them, "Men of Israel, why are you surprised? You are looking at us as if it were our own power that made this man walk. Do you think this happened because we are good? No! ¹³The God of Abraham, Isaac and Jacob, the God of our ancestors, gave glory to Jesus, his servant. But you gave him up to be killed. Pilate decided to let him go free. But you told Pilate you did not want Jesus. ¹⁴He was pure and good, but you said you did not want him. You told Pilate to give you a murderer instead of Jesus. ¹⁵And so you killed the One who gives life! But God raised him from death. We are witnesses to this. ¹⁶It was the power of Jesus that made this crippled man well. This happened because we trusted in the power of Jesus. You can see this man, and you know him. He was made completely well because of trust in Jesus. You all saw it happen!"

4:¹While Peter and John were speaking to the people, a group of men came up to them. There were Jewish priests, the captain of the soldiers that guarded the Temple, and some Sadducees. ²They were upset because the two apostles were teaching the people. Peter and John were preaching that people will rise from death through the power of Jesus. ³The Jewish leaders grabbed Peter and John and put them in jail. It was already night, so they kept them in jail until the next day. ⁴But many of those who heard Peter and John preach believed the things they said. There were now about 5,000 men in the group of believers.

Peter and John Talk to the Jewish Leaders

(From Acts 4)

4:⁵The next day the Jewish leaders . . . met in Jerusalem. ⁶Annas the high priest, Caiaphas, John, and Alexander were there. Everyone from the high priest's family was there. ⁷They made Peter and John stand before them. The Jewish leaders asked them: "By what power or authority did you do this?"

⁸Then Peter was filled with the Holy Spirit. He said to them, "Rulers of the people and you older leaders, ⁹are you questioning us about a good thing that was done to a crippled man? Are you asking us who made him well? ¹⁰We want all of you and all of the Jewish people to know that this man was made well by the power of Jesus Christ  from Nazareth! You nailed him to a cross, but God raised him from death. This man was crippled, but

he is now well and able to stand here before you because of the power of Jesus! [11]Jesus is

'the stone that you builders did not want.

It has become the cornerstone.'

[12]Jesus is the only One who can save people. His name is the only power in the world that has been given to save people. And we must be saved through him!"

[13]The Jewish leaders saw that Peter and John were not afraid to speak. They understood that these men had no special training or education. So they were amazed. Then they realized that Peter and John had been with Jesus. [14]They saw the crippled man standing there beside the two apostles. They saw that the man was healed. So they could say nothing against them. [15]The Jewish leaders told them to leave the meeting. Then the leaders talked to each other about what they should do. [16]They said, "What shall we do with these men? Everyone in Jerusalem knows that they have done a great miracle! We cannot say it is not true. [17]But we must warn them not to talk to people anymore using that name. Then this thing will not spread among the people."

[18]So they called Peter and John in again. They told them not to speak or to teach at all in the name of Jesus. [19a]But Peter and John answered them, " . . . [20]We cannot keep quiet. We must speak about what we have seen and heard." [21-22]The Jewish leaders could not find a way to punish them because all the people were praising God for what had been done. . . . So the Jewish leaders warned the apostles again and let them go free.

²³Peter and John left the meeting of Jewish leaders and went to their own group. They told them everything that the leading priests and the older Jewish leaders had said to them. ²⁴When the believers heard this, they prayed to God with one purpose. They prayed, "Lord, you are the One who made the sky, the earth, the sea, and everything in the world. ³⁰Help us to be brave by showing us your power; make sick people well, give proofs, and make miracles happen by the power of Jesus, your holy servant."

Ananias and Sapphira Lie to God
(From Acts 4 and 5)

4:³²The group of believers were joined in their hearts, and they had the same spirit. No person in the group said that the things he had were his own. Instead, they shared everything. ³³With great power the apostles were telling people that the Lord Jesus was truly raised from death. And God blessed all the believers very much. ³⁴They all received the things they needed. Everyone that owned fields or houses sold them. They brought the money ³⁵and gave it to the apostles. Then each person was given the things he needed.

³⁶One of the believers was named Joseph. The apostles called him Barnabas. (This name means "one who encourages.") He was a Levite, born in Cyprus. ³⁷Joseph owned a field. He sold it, brought the money, and gave it to the apostles.

5:¹A man named Ananias and his wife Sapphira sold some land. ²But he gave only part of the money to the apostles. He secretly kept some of it for himself. His wife knew about this, and she agreed to it. ³Peter said, "Ananias, why did you let Satan rule your heart? You lied to the Holy Spirit. Why did you keep part of the money you received for the land for yourself? ⁴Before you sold the land, it belonged to you. And even after you sold it, you could have used the money any way you wanted. Why did you think of doing this? You lied to God, not to men!" ⁵⁻⁶When Ananias heard this, he fell down and died. Some young men came in, wrapped up his body, carried it out, and buried it. And everyone who heard about this was filled with fear.

⁷About three hours later his wife came in. She did not know what had happened. ⁸Peter said to her, "Tell me how much money you got for your field. Was it this much?"

Sapphira answered, "Yes, that was the price."

⁹Peter said to her, "Why did you and your husband agree to test the Spirit of the Lord? Look! The men who buried your husband are at the door! They will carry you out." ¹⁰At that moment Sapphira fell down by his feet and died. The young men came in and saw that she was dead. They carried her out and buried her beside her husband. ¹¹The whole church and all the others who heard about these things were filled with fear.

¹²The apostles did many signs and miracles among the people. And they would all meet together on Solomon's Porch. ¹⁴More and more men and women believed in the Lord and were added to the group of believers. ¹⁵As Peter was passing by, the people brought their sick into the streets. They put their sick on beds and mats so at least Peter's shadow might fall on them. ¹⁶Crowds came from all the towns around Jerusalem. They brought their sick and those who were bothered by evil spirits. All of them were healed.

Peter and the Apostles Obey God
(From Acts 5)

5:¹⁷The high priest and all his friends (a group called the Sadducees) became very jealous. ¹⁸They took the apostles and put them in jail. ¹⁹But during the night, an angel of the Lord opened the doors of the jail. He led the apostles outside and said, ²⁰"Go and stand in the Temple. Tell the people everything about this new life." ²¹When the apostles heard this, they obeyed and went into the Temple. It was early in the morning, and they began to teach.

The high priest and his friends arrived. They called a meeting of the Jewish leaders and all the important older men of the Jews. They sent some men to the jail to bring the apostles to them. ²²ᵃWhen the men went to the jail, they could not find the apostles. ²³They said, "The jail was closed and locked. The guards were standing at the doors. But when we opened the doors, the jail was empty!"

²⁵Then someone came and told them, "Listen! The men you put in jail are standing in the Temple. They are teaching the people!" ²⁶Then the captain and his men went out and brought the apostles back. But the soldiers did not use force, because they were afraid that the people would kill them with stones.

²⁷The soldiers brought the apostles to the meeting and made them stand before the Jewish leaders.

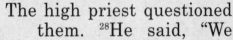

The high priest questioned them. ²⁸He said, "We gave you strict orders not to go on teaching in that name. But look what you have done! You have filled Jerusalem with your teaching. You are trying to make us responsible for this man's death."

²⁹Peter and the other apostles answered, "We must obey God, not men! ³⁰You killed Jesus. You hung him on a cross. But God . . . raised Jesus up from death! ³¹ᵇGod made Jesus our Leader and Savior. God did this so that all Jews could change their hearts and lives and have their sins forgiven. ³²We saw all these things happen. The Holy Spirit also proves that these things are true. God has given the Spirit to all who obey him."

³³When the Jewish leaders heard this, they became very angry and wanted to kill them. ³⁴A Pharisee

named Gamaliel stood up in the meeting. He was a teacher of the law, and all the people respected him. He ordered the apostles to leave the meeting for a little while. ³⁵Then he said to them, "Men of Israel, be careful of what you are planning to do to these men!"

⁴⁰[The Jewish leaders] called the apostles in again. They beat the apostles and told them not to speak in the name of Jesus again. Then they let them go free. ⁴¹The apostles left the meeting full of joy because they were given the honor of suffering disgrace for Jesus. ⁴²The apostles did not stop teaching people. Every day in the Temple and in people's homes they continued to tell the Good News—that Jesus is the Christ.

Stephen Is Arrested

(From Acts 6 and 7)

6:⁸ Stephen was richly blessed by God. God gave him the power to do great miracles and signs among the people. ⁹But some Jews were against him. They belonged to a synagogue of Free Men (as it was called). (This synagogue was also for Jews from Cyrene and from Alexandria.) Jews from Cilicia and Asia were also with them. They all came and argued with Stephen.

¹⁰But the Spirit was helping him to speak with wisdom. His words were so strong that they could not argue with him. ¹¹So they paid some men to say, "We heard him say things against Moses and against God!"

¹²This upset the people, the older Jewish leaders, and the teachers of the law. They came to Stephen, grabbed him and brought him to a meeting of the Jewish leaders. ¹³They brought in some men to tell lies about Stephen. They said, "This man is always saying things against this holy place and the law of Moses. ¹⁴We heard him say that Jesus from Nazareth will destroy this place. He also said that Jesus will change the things that Moses told us to do." ¹⁵All the people in the meeting were watching Stephen closely. His face looked like the face of an angel.

7:⁵¹Stephen [said], "You stubborn Jewish leaders! You have not given your hearts to God! You won't listen to him! You are always against what the Holy Spirit is trying to tell you. Your ancestors were like this, and you are just like them! ⁵²Your fathers tried to hurt every prophet who ever lived. Those prophets said long ago that the Righteous One would come. But your fathers killed them. And now you have turned against the Righteous One and killed him. ⁵³You received the law of Moses, which God gave you through his angels. But you don't obey it!"

⁵⁴When the leaders heard Stephen saying all these things, they became very angry. They were so mad that they were grinding their teeth at Stephen. ⁵⁵But Stephen was full of the Holy Spirit. He looked up to heaven and saw the glory of God. He saw Jesus standing at God's right side. ⁵⁶He said, "Look! I see heaven open. And I see the Son of Man standing at God's right side!"

⁵⁷Then they all shouted loudly. They covered their ears with their hands and all ran at Stephen. ⁵⁸They took him out of the city and threw stones at him until he was dead. The men who told lies against Stephen left their coats with a young man named Saul. ⁵⁹While they were throwing stones, Stephen prayed, "Lord Jesus, receive my spirit!" ⁶⁰He fell

on his knees and cried in a loud voice, "Lord, do not hold this sin against them!" After Stephen said this, he died.

Philip Teaches
the Ethiopian Officer

(From Acts 8)

8:¹Saul agreed that the killing of Stephen was a good thing.

²⁻³Some religious men buried Stephen. They cried very loudly for him. On that day people began trying to hurt the church in Jerusalem and make it suffer. Saul was also trying to destroy the church. He went from house to house. He dragged out men and women and put them in jail. All the believers, except the apostles, went to different places in Judea and Samaria. ⁴And everywhere

they were scattered, they told people the Good News.

⁵Philip went to the city of Samaria and preached about the Christ. ⁶The people there heard Philip and saw the miracles he was doing. They all listened carefully to the things he said. ⁷Many of these people had evil spirits in them. But Philip made the evil spirits leave them. The spirits made a loud noise when they came out. There were also many weak and crippled people there. Philip healed them, too. ⁸So the people in that city were very happy.

²⁶An angel of the Lord spoke to Philip. The angel said, "Get ready and go south. Go to the road that leads down to Gaza from Jerusalem—the desert road." ²⁷So Philip got ready and went. On the road he saw a man from Ethiopia. . . . He was an important officer in the service of Candace, the queen of the Ethiopians. He was responsible for taking care of all her money. He had gone to Jerusalem to worship, and ²⁸now he was on his way home. He was sitting in his chariot and reading from the book of Isaiah, the prophet. ²⁹The Spirit said to Philip, "Go to that chariot and stay near it."

³⁰So Philip ran toward the chariot. He heard the man reading from Isaiah, the prophet. Philip asked, "Do you understand what you are reading?"

³¹He answered, "How can I understand? I need someone to explain it to me!" Then he invited Philip to climb in and sit with him. ³²The verse of Scripture that he was reading was this:

"He was like a sheep being led to be killed.
　He was quiet, as a sheep is quiet while its wool
　　is being cut.
He said nothing.
³³　He was shamed and was treated unfairly.
He died without children to continue his family.
　His life on earth has ended."

³⁴The officer said to Philip, "Please tell me, who is the prophet talking about? Is he talking about himself or about someone else?" ³⁵Philip began to speak. He started with this same Scripture and told the man the Good News about Jesus.

³⁶While they were traveling down the road, they came to some water. The officer said, "Look! Here is water! What is stopping me from being baptized?" ³⁸Then the officer commanded the chariot to stop. Both Philip and the officer went down into the water, and Philip baptized him. ³⁹When they came up out of the water, the Spirit of the Lord took Philip away; the officer never saw him again. The officer continued on his way home, full of joy.

Saul Meets Jesus on the Road to Damascus

(From Acts 9)

9:¹In Jerusalem Saul was still trying to frighten the followers of the Lord by saying he would kill them. So he went to the high priest ²and asked him to write letters to the synagogues in the city of Damascus. Saul wanted the high priest to give him the authority to find people in Damascus who were followers of Christ's Way. If he found any there, men or women, he would arrest them and bring them back to Jerusalem.

³So Saul went to Damascus. As he came near the city, a bright light from heaven suddenly flashed around him. ⁴Saul fell to the ground. He heard a voice saying to him, "Saul, Saul! Why are you doing things against me?"

⁵Saul said, "Who are you, Lord?"

The voice answered, "I am Jesus. I am the One you are trying to hurt. ⁶Get up now and go into the city. Someone there will tell you what you must do."

⁷The men traveling with Saul stood there, but they said nothing. They heard the voice, but they saw no one. ⁸Saul got up from the ground. He opened his eyes, but he could not see. So the men with Saul took his hand and led him into Damascus. ⁹For three days Saul could not see, and he did not eat or drink.

¹⁰There was a follower of Jesus in Damascus named Ananias. The Lord spoke to Ananias in a vision, "Ananias!"

Ananias answered, "Here I am, Lord."

¹¹The Lord said to him, "Get up and go to the street called Straight Street. Find the house of Judas. Ask for a man named Saul from the city of Tarsus. He is there now, praying. ¹²Saul has seen a vision. In it a man named Ananias comes to him and lays his hands on him. Then he sees again."

¹³But Ananias answered, "Lord, many people have told me about this man and the terrible things he did to your people in Jerusalem. ¹⁴Now he has come here to Damascus. The leading priests have given him the power to arrest everyone who worships you."

¹⁵But the Lord said to Ananias, "Go! I have chosen Saul for an important work. He must tell about me to non-Jews, to kings, and to the people of Israel. ¹⁶I will show him how much he must suffer for my name."

¹⁷So Ananias went to the house of Judas. He laid his hands on Saul and said, "Brother Saul, the Lord Jesus sent me. He is the one you saw on the road on your way here. He sent me so that you can see again and be filled with the Holy Spirit." ¹⁸Immediately, something that looked like fish scales fell from Saul's eyes. He was able to see again! Then Saul got up and was baptized.

¹⁹ᵇSaul stayed with the followers of Jesus in Damascus for a few days. ²⁰Soon he began to preach about Jesus in the synagogues, saying, "Jesus is the Son of God!"

Peter Teaches Cornelius

(From Acts 10)

10:¹At Caesarea there was a man named Cornelius. He was an officer in the Italian group of the Roman army. ²Cornelius was a religious man. He and all the other people who lived in his house worshiped the true God. He gave much of his money to the poor and prayed to God often. ³One afternoon about three o'clock, Cornelius saw a vision clearly. In the vision an angel of God came to him and said, "Cornelius!"

⁴Cornelius stared at the angel. He became afraid and said, "What do you want, Lord?"

The angel said, "God has heard your prayers. He has seen what you give to the poor. And God remembers you. ⁵Send some men now to Joppa to bring back a man named Simon. Simon is also called Peter." ⁷ᵃThen the angel who spoke to Cornelius left. Cornelius called two of his servants and a soldier. ⁸Cornelius explained everything to these three men and sent them to Joppa.

⁹The next day as they came near Joppa, Peter was going up to the roof to pray. It was about noon. ¹⁰Peter was hungry and wanted to eat. But while the food was being

prepared, he had a vision. ¹¹He saw heaven opened and something coming down. It looked like a big sheet being lowered to earth by its four corners. ¹²In it were all kinds of animals, reptiles, and birds. ¹³Then a voice said to Peter, "Get up, Peter; kill and eat."

¹⁴But Peter said, 'No, Lord! I have never eaten food that is unholy or unclean."

¹⁵But the voice said to him again, "God has made these things clean. Don't call them 'unholy'!" ¹⁶This happened three times. Then the sheet was taken back to heaven.

¹⁷While Peter was wondering what this vision meant, the men Cornelius sent had found Simon's house. They were standing at the gate. ¹⁸They asked, "Is Simon Peter staying here?"

¹⁹Peter was still thinking about the vision. But the Spirit said to him, "Listen! Three men are looking for you. ²⁰Get up and go downstairs. Go with them and don't ask questions. I have sent them to you."

²³ᵇThe next day Peter got ready and went with them. Some of the brothers from Joppa joined him. ²⁴On the following day they came to Caesarea. Cornelius was waiting for them. He had called together his relatives and close friends.

³⁴Peter began to speak: "I really understand now that to God every person is the same. ³⁵ᵃGod accepts anyone who worships him and does what is right.⁴³ᵃEveryone who believes in Jesus will be forgiven. God will forgive his sins through Jesus."

⁴⁴While Peter was still saying this, the Holy Spirit came down on all those who were listening.

⁴⁵The Jewish believers who came with Peter were amazed that the gift of the Holy Spirit had been given even to the non-Jewish people. ⁴⁶ᵇThen Peter said, ⁴⁷"Can anyone keep these people from being baptized with water? They have received the Holy Spirit just as we did!"

Peter's Chains Fall Off

(From Acts 12)

12:¹During that same time King Herod began to do terrible things to some who belonged to the church. ²He ordered James, the brother of John, to be killed by the sword. ³Herod saw that the Jews liked this, so he decided to arrest Peter, too. (This happened during the time of the Feast of Unleavened Bread.)

⁴After Herod arrested Peter, he put him in jail and handed him over to be guarded by 16 soldiers. Herod planned to bring Peter before the people for trial after the Passover Feast. ⁵So Peter was kept in jail. But the church kept on praying to God for him.

⁶The night before Herod was to bring him to trial, Peter was sleeping. He was between two soldiers, bound with two chains. Other soldiers were guarding the door of the jail. ⁷Suddenly, an angel of the Lord stood there. A light shined in the room. The angel touched Peter on the side and woke him up. The angel said, "Hurry! Get up!" And the

chains fell off Peter's hands. [8]The angel said to
him, "Get dressed and put on your sandals." And
so Peter did this. Then the angel said, "Put on
your coat and follow me." [9]So the angel went out,
and Peter followed him. Peter did not know if
what the angel was doing was real. He thought he
might be seeing a vision. [10]They went past the first

and the second guard. They came to the iron gate that separated them from the city. The gate opened itself for them. They went through the gate and walked down a street. And the angel suddenly left him.

[11]Then Peter realized what had happened. He thought, "Now I know that the Lord really sent his angel to me. He rescued me from Herod and from all the things the Jewish people thought would happen."

[12]When he realized this, he went to the home of Mary. She was the mother of John. (John was also called Mark.) Many people were gathered there, praying. [13]Peter knocked on the outside door. A servant girl named Rhoda came to answer it. [14]She recognized Peter's voice, and she was very happy. She even forgot to open the door. She ran inside and told the group, "Peter is at the door!"

[15]They said to her, "You are crazy!" But she kept on saying that it was true. So they said, "It must be Peter's angel."

[16]Peter continued to knock. When they opened the door, they saw him and were amazed. [17]Peter made a sign with his hand to tell them to be quiet. He explained how the Lord led him out of the jail. And he said, "Tell James and the other believers what happened." Then he left to go to another place.

[18]The next day the soldiers were very upset. They wondered what had happened to Peter. [19]Herod looked everywhere for Peter but could not find him. So he questioned the guards and ordered that they be killed.

Paul and Barnabas Tell
the Good News

(From Acts 13—15)

13:¹In the church at Antioch there were these prophets and teachers: Barnabas, Simeon . . . , Lucius . . . , Manaen . . . and Saul. ²They were all worshiping the Lord and giving up eating. The Holy Spirit said to them, "Give Barnabas and Saul to me to do a special work. I have chosen them for it."

³So they gave up eating and prayed. They laid their hands on Barnabas and Saul and sent them out.

⁴ᵃBarnabas and Saul were sent out by the Holy Spirit.

14:⁸In Lystra there sat a man who had been born crippled; he had never walked. ⁹This man was listening to Paul speak. Paul looked straight at him and saw that the man believed God could heal him. ¹⁰So he cried out, "Stand up on your feet!" The man jumped up and began walking around. ¹¹When the crowds saw what Paul did, they shouted in their own Lycaonian language. They said, "The gods have become like men! They have come down to us!" ¹³The temple of Zeus was near the city. The priest of this temple brought some bulls and flowers to the city gates. The priest and the people

wanted to offer a sacrifice to Paul and Barnabas.
[14]But when the apostles, Barnabas and Paul,
understood what they were about to do, they tore
their clothes in anger. Then they ran in among the
people and shouted, [15]"Men, why are you doing
these things? We are only men, human beings like
you! . . . We are telling you to turn . . . to the true
living God. He is the One who made the sky, the
earth, the sea, and everything that is in them. [16]In
the past, God let all the nations do what they
wanted. [17]Yet he did things to prove he is real: He
shows kindness to you. He gives you rain from
heaven and crops at the right times. He gives you
food and fills your hearts with joy." [18]Even with
these words, they were barely able to keep the
crowd from offering sacrifices to them.

[19]Then some Jews came from Antioch and
Iconium. They persuaded the people to turn
against Paul. And so they threw stones at Paul and
dragged him out of town. They thought that they
had killed him. [20]But the followers gathered
around him, and he got up and went back into the
town. The next day, he and Barnabas left and went
to the city of Derbe.

15:[36]After some time, Paul said to Barnabas, "We
preached the message of the Lord in many towns.
We should go back to all those towns to visit the
believers and see how they are doing."

[37]Barnabas wanted to take John Mark with them
too. [38]But John Mark had left them at Pamphylia;
he did not continue with them in the work. So
Paul did not think it was a good idea to take him.

[39]Paul and Barnabas had a serious argument about this. They separated and went different ways. Barnabas sailed to Cyprus and took Mark with him. [40]But Paul chose Silas and left. The believers in Antioch put Paul into the Lord's care.

Paul and Silas in Jail

(From Acts 16)

16:[16]Once, while we were going to the place for prayer, a servant girl met us. She had a special spirit in her. She earned a lot of money for her owners by telling fortunes. [17]This girl followed Paul and us. She said loudly, "These men are servants of the Most High God! They are telling you how you can be saved!"

[18]She kept this up for many days. This bothered Paul, so he turned and said to the spirit, "By the power of Jesus Christ, I command you to come out of her!" Immediately, the spirit came out.

[19]The owners of the servant girl saw this. These men knew that now they could not use her to make money. So they grabbed Paul and Silas and dragged them before the city rulers in the marketplace. [20]Here they brought Paul and Silas to the Roman rulers and said, "These men are Jews and are making trouble in our city. [21]They are teaching things that are not right for us as Romans to do."

[22]The crowd joined the attack against them. The Roman officers tore the clothes of Paul and Silas

and had them beaten with rods again and again. ²³Then Paul and Silas were thrown into jail. The jailer was ordered to guard them carefully. ²⁴When he heard this order, he put them far inside the jail. He pinned down their feet between large blocks of wood.

²⁵About midnight Paul and Silas were praying and singing songs to God. The other prisoners were listening to them. ²⁶Suddenly, there was a big earthquake. It was so strong that it shook the foundation of the jail. Then all the doors of the jail broke open. All the prisoners were freed from their chains. ²⁷The jailer woke up and saw that the jail doors were open. He thought that the prisoners had already escaped. So he got his sword and was about to kill himself. ²⁸But Paul shouted, "Don't hurt yourself! We are all here!"

²⁹The jailer told someone to bring a light. Then he ran inside. Shaking with fear, he fell down before Paul and Silas. ³⁰Then he brought them outside and said, "Men, what must I do to be saved?"

³¹They said to him, "Believe in the Lord Jesus and you will be saved—you and all the people in your house." ³²So Paul and Silas told the message of the Lord to the jailer and all the people in his house. ³³At that hour of the night the jailer took Paul and Silas and washed their wounds. Then he and all his people were baptized immediately. ³⁴After this

the jailer took Paul and Silas home and gave them food. He and his family were very happy because they now believed in God.

Paul Goes to Jerusalem

(From Acts 21)

21:[7]We continued our trip from Tyre and arrived at Ptolemais. We greeted the believers there and stayed with them for a day. [8]We left Ptolemais and went to the city of Caesarea. There we went into the home of Philip and stayed with him. Philip had the work of telling the Good News. He was one of the seven helpers. [9]He had four unmarried daughters who had the gift of prophesying. [10]After we had been there for some time, a prophet named Agabus arrived from Judea. [11]He came to us and borrowed Paul's belt. Then he used the belt to tie his own hands and feet. He said, "The Holy Spirit says, 'This is how the Jews in Jerusalem will tie up the man who wears this belt. Then they will give him to the non-Jewish people.'"

[12]We all heard these words. So we and the people there begged Paul not to go to Jerusalem. [13]But he said, "Why are you crying and making me so sad? I am ready to be tied up in Jerusalem. And I am ready to die for the Lord Jesus!"

[14]We could not persuade him to stay away from Jerusalem. So we stopped begging him and said, "We pray that what the Lord wants will be done."

[15]After this, we got ready and started on our way

to Jerusalem. ¹⁶ᵃSome of the followers from Caesarea went with us. They took us to the home of Mnason, a man from Cyprus.

¹⁷In Jerusalem the believers were glad to see us. ¹⁸The next day, Paul went with us to visit James. All the elders were there, too. ¹⁹Paul greeted them and told them everything that God had done among the non-Jewish people through him.

²⁶ᵃ . . . The next day, ²⁷ᵇ . . . some Jews from Asia saw Paul at the Temple. They caused all the people to be upset, and they grabbed Paul. ²⁸ᵃThey shouted, "Men of Israel, help us! This is the man who goes everywhere teaching things that are against the law of Moses, against our people, and against this Temple."

³⁰All the people in Jerusalem became very upset. They ran and took Paul and dragged him out of the Temple. The Temple doors were closed immediately. ³¹The people were about to kill Paul. Now the commander of the Roman army in Jerusalem learned that there was trouble in the whole city. ³²Immediately he ran to the place where the crowd was gathered. He brought officers and soldiers with him, and the people saw them. So they stopped beating Paul. ³³The commander went to Paul and arrested him. He told his soldiers to tie Paul with two chains. Then he asked, "Who is this man? What has he done wrong?" ³⁴Some in the crowd were yelling one thing, and some were yelling

another. Because of all this confusion and shouting, the commander could not learn what had happened. So he ordered the soldiers to take Paul to the army building.

Paul Is Arrested in Jerusalem
(From Acts 21 and 22)

21:³⁷ The soldiers were about to take Paul into the army building. But he spoke to the commander, "May I say something to you?"

The commander said, "Do you speak Greek? ³⁸I thought you were the Egyptian who started some trouble against the government not long ago. He led 4,000 killers out to the desert."

³⁹Paul said, "No, I am a Jew from Tarsus in the country of Cilicia. I am a citizen of that important city. Please, let me speak to the people."

⁴⁰The commander gave permission, so Paul stood on the steps. He waved with his hand so that the people would be quiet. When there was silence, Paul spoke to them in the Jewish language.

22:¹ Paul said, "Brothers and fathers, listen to me! I will make my defense to you." ²When the Jews heard him speaking the Jewish language, they became very quiet. Paul said, ³"I am a Jew. I was born in Tarsus in the country of Cilicia. I grew up in this city. I was a student of Gamaliel. He carefully taught me everything about the law of our ancestors. I was very serious about serving God, just as are all of you here today. ⁴I hurt the people who followed the Way of Jesus. Some of them were even killed. I arrested men and women and put them in jail. ⁵The high priest and the whole council of older Jewish leaders can tell you that this is true. These leaders gave me letters to the Jewish brothers in Damascus. So I was going there to arrest these people and bring them back to Jerusalem to be punished.

⁶"But something happened to me on my way to Damascus. It was about noon when I came near Damascus. Suddenly a bright light from heaven flashed all around me. ⁷I fell to the ground and heard a voice saying, 'Saul, Saul, why are you doing things against me?' ⁸I asked, 'Who are you, Lord?' The voice said, 'I am Jesus from Nazareth. I am the One you are trying to hurt.' ¹⁰I said, 'What shall I do, Lord?' The Lord answered, 'Get up and go to Damascus. There you will be told about all the things I have planned for you to do.'

¹²ᵃ"There a man named Ananaias came to me. ¹⁴Ananias told me, 'The God of our fathers chose you long ago. He chose you to know his plan. He chose you to see the Righteous One and to hear words from him. ¹⁵You will be his witness to all people. You will tell them about the things you have seen and heard.'

¹⁷ᵃ"Later I returned to Jerusalem. ²¹But the Lord said to me, 'Leave now. I will send you far away to the non-Jewish people.'"

²²ᵃThe crowd listened to

Paul until he said this. Then they began shouting, "Kill him!"

²⁴ªThen the commander ordered the soldiers to take Paul into the army building. . . .

The Plot Against Paul

(From Acts 23 and 24)

23:¹²In the morning some of the Jews made a plan to kill Paul. They made a promise that they would not eat or drink anything until they had killed him. ¹³There were more than 40 Jews who made this plan. ¹⁴They went and talked to the leading priests and the older Jewish leaders. They said, "We have made a promise to ourselves that we will not eat or drink until we have killed Paul! ¹⁵So this is what we want you to do: Send a message to the commander to bring Paul out to you. Tell him you want to ask Paul more questions. We will be waiting to kill him while he is on the way here."

¹⁶But Paul's nephew heard about this plan. He went to the army building and told Paul about it. ¹⁷Then Paul called one of the officers and said, "Take this young man to the commander. He has a message for him."

¹⁸So the officer brought Paul's nephew to the commander. The officer said, "The prisoner, Paul, asked me to bring this young man to you. He wants to tell you something."

¹⁹The commander led the young man to a place

where they could be alone. The commander asked, "What do you want to tell me?"

²⁰The young man said, "The Jews have decided to ask you to bring Paul down to their council meeting tomorrow. They want you to think that they are going to ask him more questions. ²¹But don't believe them! There are more than 40 men who are hiding and waiting to kill Paul. They have all made a promise not to eat or drink until they have killed him! Now they are waiting for you to agree."

²²The commander sent the young man away. He said to him, "Don't tell anyone that you have told me about their plan."

²³Then the commander called two officers. He said to them, "I need some men to go to Caesarea. Get 200 soldiers ready. Also, get 70 horsemen and 200 men with spears. Be ready to leave at nine o'clock tonight. ²⁴Get some horses for Paul to ride. He must be taken to Governor Felix safely."

³¹So the soldiers did what they were told. They took Paul and brought him to the city of Antipatris that night. ³²ᵃThe next day the horsemen went with Paul to Caesarea. ³⁴The governor . . . asked Paul, "What area are you from?" He learned that Paul was from Cilicia. ³⁵ᵃHe said, "I will hear your case when those who are against you come here too." Then the governor gave orders for Paul to be kept under guard in the palace.

24:²³ᵇ But [Felix] told the officer to give Paul some freedom and to let his friends bring what he needed.

²⁷ . . . After two years, Porcius Festus became governor. Felix was no longer governor, but he had left Paul in prison to please the Jews.

Paul Is Shipwrecked

(From Acts 25, 27, and 28)

25:¹ Three days after Festus became governor, he went from Caesarea to Jerusalem. ²There the leading priests and the important Jewish leaders made charges against Paul before Festus.

⁶Festus stayed in Jerusalem another eight or ten days. Then he went back to Caesarea. The next day he told the soldiers to bring Paul before him. Festus was seated on the judge's seat ⁷ᵃwhen Paul came into the room.

⁹ . . . Festus wanted to please the Jews. So he asked Paul, "Do you want to go to Jerusalem? Do you want me to judge you there on these charges?"

¹⁰ᵃPaul said, "I am standing at Caesar's judgment seat now. ¹¹ᵇNo! I want Caesar to hear my case!"

27:¹ᵃ It was decided that we would sail for Italy. ⁷ᵃWe sailed slowly for many days.

¹³ᵃThen a good wind began to blow from the south. ¹⁴ᵃBut then a very strong wind named the "Northeaster" came. . . . ¹⁵This wind took the ship and carried it away. The ship could not sail against it. So we stopped trying and let the wind blow us.

[18]The next day the storm was blowing us so hard that the men threw out some of the cargo. [19]A day later they threw out the ship's equipment. [20]For many days we could not see the sun or the stars. The storm was very bad. We lost all hope of staying alive—we thought we would die.

[21a]The men had gone without food for a long time. Then one day Paul stood up before them and said, " . . . [22]But now I tell you to cheer up. None of you will die! But the ship will be lost. [23a]Last night an angel from God came to me. [24]God's angel said, 'Paul, do not be afraid! You must stand before Caesar. And God has given you this promise: He will save the lives of all those men sailing with you.' [25]So men, be cheerful! I trust in God. Everything will happen as his angel told me. [26]But we will crash on an island."

[39]When daylight came, the sailors saw land. . . . They wanted to sail the ship to the beach, if they could. [40]So they cut the ropes to the anchors and . . . they untied the ropes that were holding the rudders. Then they raised the front sail into the wind and sailed toward the beach. [41]But the ship hit a sandbank. The front of the ship stuck there and could not move. Then the big waves began to break the back of the ship to pieces.

[42]The soldiers decided to kill the prisoners so that none of them could swim away and escape. [43]But Julius, the officer, wanted to let Paul live. He did not allow the soldiers to kill

the prisoners. Instead he ordered everyone who could swim to jump into the water and swim to land. ⁴⁴The rest used wooden boards or pieces of the ship. And this is how all the people made it safely to land.

28:¹ When we were safe on land, we learned that the island was called Malta.

Paul in Rome

(From Acts 28)

28:² It was raining and very cold. But the people who lived [on the island of Malta] were very good to us. They made us a fire and welcomed all of us. ³Paul gathered a pile of sticks for the fire. He was putting them on the fire when a poisonous snake came out because of the heat and bit him on the hand. ⁵But Paul shook the snake off into the fire. He was not hurt. ⁶ᵃThe people thought that Paul would swell up or fall down dead. The people waited and watched him for a long time, but nothing bad happened to him.

¹⁰⁻¹¹The people on the island gave us many honors. We stayed there three months. When we were ready to leave, they gave us the things we needed. We got on a ship from Alexandria. The ship had stayed on the island during the winter. . . . ¹⁴ᵇFinally, we came to Rome. ¹⁵The believers in Rome heard that we were there. They came out . . . to meet us. When Paul saw them, he was encouraged and thanked God.

[In] Rome . . . Paul was allowed to live alone. But a soldier stayed with him to guard him.

[17]Three days later Paul sent for the Jewish leaders there. When they came together, he said, "Brothers, I have done nothing against our people. I have done nothing against the customs of our fathers. But I was arrested in Jerusalem and given to the Romans. [18]The Romans asked me many questions. But they could find no reason why I should be killed. They wanted to let me go free, [19]but the Jews there did not want that. So I had to ask to come to Rome to have my trial before Caesar. But I have no charge to bring against my own people. [20]That is why I wanted to see you and talk with you. I am bound with this chain because I believe in the hope of Israel."

[21]The Jews answered Paul, "We have received no letters from Judea about you. None of our Jewish brothers who have come from there brought news about you or told us anything bad about you. [22]We want to hear your ideas. We know that people everywhere are speaking against this religious group."

[23]Paul and the Jews chose a day for a meeting. On that day many more of the Jews met with Paul at the place he was staying. Paul spoke to them all day long, explaining the kingdom of God to them. He tried to persuade them to believe these things about Jesus. He used the law of Moses and the writings of the prophets to do this.

[30]Paul stayed two full years in his own rented

house. He welcomed all people who came and visited him. ³¹He preached about the kingdom of God and taught about the Lord Jesus Christ. He was very bold, and no one tried to stop him from speaking.

John on the Island of Patmos
(From Revelation 1 and 7)

1:⁹I am John, and I am your brother in Christ. . . . I was on the island of Patmos because I had preached God's message and the truth about Jesus. ¹⁰On the Lord's day the Spirit took control of me. I heard a loud voice behind me that sounded like a trumpet. ¹¹The voice said, "Write what you see and send that book to the seven churches: to Ephesus, Smyrna, Pergamum, Thyatira, Sardis, Philadelphia, and Laodicea."

¹²I turned to see who was talking to me. When I turned, I saw seven golden lampstands. ¹³I saw someone among the lampstands who was "like a Son of Man." He was dressed in a long robe. He had a gold band around his chest. ¹⁴His head and hair were white like wool, as white as snow. His eyes were like flames of fire. ¹⁵His feet were like bronze that glows hot in a furnace. His voice was like the noise of flooding water. ¹⁶He held seven stars in his right hand. A sharp two-edged sword came out of his mouth. He looked like the sun shining at its brightest time.

¹⁷When I saw him, I fell down at his feet like a

dead man. He put his right hand on me and said, "Do not be afraid! I am the First and the Last. [18]I am the One who lives. I was dead, but look: I am alive forever and ever! And I hold the keys of death and where the dead are."

7:[9]Then I looked, and there was a great number of people. There were so many people that no one could count them. They were from every nation, tribe, people, and language of the earth. They were all standing before the throne and before the Lamb. They wore white robes and had palm branches in their hands. [10]They were shouting in a loud voice, "Salvation belongs to our God, who sits on the throne, and to the Lamb." [11]The elders and the four living things were there. All the angels were standing around them and the throne. The angels bowed down on their faces before the throne and worshiped God. [12]They were saying, "Amen! Praise, glory, wisdom, thanks, honor, power, and strength belong to our God forever and ever. Amen!"

[14b]And the elder said, "These are the people who have come out of the great suffering. They have washed their robes with the blood of the Lamb. Now they are clean and white. [15]And they are before the throne of God. They worship God day and night in his temple. And the One who sits on

the throne will protect them. ¹⁶Those people will never be hungry again. They will never be thirsty again. The sun will not hurt them. No heat will burn them. ¹⁷For the Lamb at the center of the throne will be their shepherd. He will lead them to springs of water that give life. And God will wipe away every tear from their eyes."

The King of Kings

(From Revelation 19, 21, and 22)

19:¹¹Then I [John] saw heaven open. There before me was a white horse. The rider on the horse is called Faithful and True. He is right when he judges and makes war. ¹²His eyes are like burning fire, and on his head are many crowns. He has a name written on him, but he is the only one who

knows the name. No other person knows the name. ¹³He is dressed in a robe dipped in blood. His name is the Word of God. ¹⁴The armies of heaven were following him on white horses. They were dressed in fine linen, white and clean. ¹⁵A sharp sword comes out of the rider's mouth. He will use this sword to defeat the nations. He will rule them with a scepter of iron. He will crush out the wine in the winepress of the terrible anger of God All-Powerful. ¹⁶On his robe and on his leg was written this name: "KING OF KINGS AND LORD OF LORDS."

21:¹Then I saw a new heaven and a new earth. The first heaven and the first earth had disappeared. Now there was no sea. ²And I saw the holy city coming down out of heaven from God. This holy city is the new Jerusalem. It was prepared like a bride dressed for her husband. ³I heard a loud voice from the throne. The voice said, "Now God's home is with men. He will live with them, and they will be his people. God himself will be with them and will be their God. ⁴He will wipe away every tear from their eyes. There will be no more death, sadness, crying, or pain. All the old ways are gone."

¹⁰The angel carried me away by the Spirit to a very large and high mountain. He showed me the holy city, Jerusalem. It was coming down out of heaven from God. ¹¹It was shining with the glory of God. It was shining bright like a very expensive jewel, like a jasper. It was clear as crystal.

22:¹²"Listen! I am coming soon! I will bring rewards with me. I will repay each one for what he has done. ¹³I am the Alpha and the Omega, the First and the Last, the Beginning and the End.

¹⁶"I, Jesus, have sent my angel to tell you these things for the churches. I am the descendant from the family of David. I am the bright morning star."

¹⁷The Spirit and the bride say, "Come!" Everyone who hears this should also say, "Come!" If anyone is thirsty, let him come; whoever wishes it may have the water of life as a free gift.

²⁰Jesus is the One who says that these things are true. Now he says, "Yes, I am coming soon."

Amen. Come, Lord Jesus!

²¹The grace of the Lord Jesus be with all. Amen.

God is always ready to listen to you when
you are happy, when you have done
wrong, and when you need his help.
But did you know that he *especially* loves
to hear you say, "Thank you, God"?
On each page of "My Bedtime Prayer,"
you'll find a place to write some
of your own thoughts about things
you're thankful for. On the "angels"
("A" page), for example, you might write:
Apples, Aunts, Armadillos.
On the "Bible" ("B" page),
you might write:
Baseball, Bananas, Books.

**Enjoy learning to thank God,
and he will make your life
happier as you pray!**

My Bedtime Prayer

Dear God, who watches over me,
Protect and bless
my sleep tonight.
Keep me safe and unafraid
Until I see tomorrow's light.
But now before I close my eyes,
I thank you for so many things
That fill our world
with happiness—
That make us smile
and laugh and sing:

I thank you for your **angels**
Who guard me
as I work and play.

A_____

_____

_____

_____

_____

_____

_____

_____

_____

_____

I thank you for the **Bible**
That guides me
on your chosen way.

B_____

_____

_____

_____

_____

_____

_____

_____

_____

_____

Dear God, I thank you
for the church—
A group where **Christians**
learn and grow.

C_____

_____

_____

_____

_____

_____

_____

_____

_____

_____

_____

324

I thank you for **direction**
And that you care
which way I go.

D _____

_____

_____

_____

_____

_____

_____

_____

_____

_____

I thank you, God,
for **eyes** to see
And **ears** to hear
the world you've made.

E_____

_____

_____

_____

_____

_____

_____

_____

_____

I thank you for my **family**
And **friends** to share
with every day.

F_____

_____

_____

_____

_____

_____

_____

_____

_____

_____

For **goals** to reach . . .
For **hills** to climb . . .

G_____

_____

_____

_____

_____

H_____

_____

_____

_____

_____

328

For **ice** to skate . . .
For **jumping** time . . .
Dear God, I thank you!

I _____

_____

_____

_____

J _____

_____

_____

_____

I thank you for your **kindness**
And that you want me to be
kind.

I thank you mostly for your **love**
And that I'm always on your
mind.

K_____

_____

_____

L_____

_____

M_____

_____

I thank you, God,
for each **new** day—
New things to see
and learn and do.
(Help me remember,
though, dear God,
There's much to learn
from **old** folks, too.)

N_____
_____
_____
_____

O_____
_____
_____

I thank you that you
hear my **prayers**
In noisy times and **quiet** ones.

P_____

_____

_____

_____

_____

_____

Q_____

_____

_____

_____

_____

332

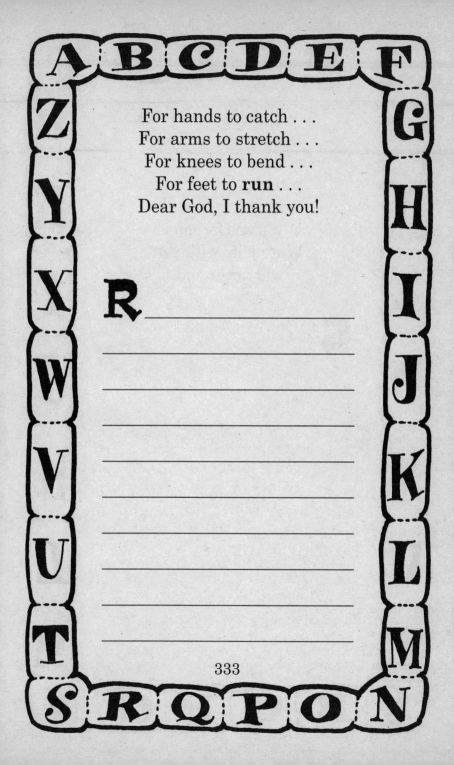

For hands to catch . . .
For arms to stretch . . .
For knees to bend . . .
For feet to **run** . . .
Dear God, I thank you!

R_____

_____

_____

_____

_____

_____

_____

_____

_____

333

I thank you that
you sent your **Son**
To save my soul
from death and sin
And that he's made
a place for me
Where life with you
will never end.

S_____

_____

_____

_____

_____

_____

_____

_____

I thank you for your **truth**,
dear God,
For **understanding,** too;
For **values** that you're
teaching me;
For **wisdom** straight from you.

T_____

_____

U_____

_____

V_____

_____

W_____

335

Excite me with your
"ex"cellence—
That I can know **you**
and your ways.
For all these things
and **zillions** more,
Dear God, I offer up my praise.
AMEN.

X _____

_____

_____

Y _____

_____

Z _____

_____

Each day, try to think
of at least one new thing
for which you should say
"thank you."
Here are just a few more ideas:

for mothers, fathers, brothers,
sisters, grandparents, aunts,
uncles, cousins; for teachers,
preachers, police officers,
firefighters, doctors, nurses;
for pets; for children
who are just like you;
for children who are
different from you;
for people who are sick or hungry
or who need special help;
for enemies, as well as for friends;
for games and toys and sports
you enjoy; for foods you
like to eat.

We have *so very many* good
and wonderful things to be
thankful for!

337